Beyond the
Schoolhouse Gate

Robert Wheeler Lane

Beyond the Schoolhouse Gate

Free Speech and the Inculcation of Values

Temple University Press · Philadelphia

Temple University Press, Philadelphia 19122
Copyright © 1995 by Temple University. All rights reserved
Published 1995
Printed in the United States of America

The paper used in this publication meets the minimum requirements of
American National Standard for Information Sciences — Permanence
of Paper for Printed Library Materials,
ANSI Z39.48-1984 ⊗

Library of Congress Cataloging-in-Publication Data
Lane, Robert Wheeler, 1954–
    Beyond the schoolhouse gate : free speech and the inculcation of
values / Robert Wheeler Lane.
        p.   cm.
    Includes bibliographical references and index.
    ISBN 1-56639-274-8 (alk. paper). — ISBN 1-56639-275-6
(pbk. : alk. paper)
    1. School discipline — United States.   2. Students — United
States — Legal status, laws, etc.   3. Freedom of speech — United
States.   4. School management and organization — United States.
5. Classroom management — United States.   I. Title.
LB3012.2.L36   1995
    371.5′0973 — dc20   94-16430

Contents

Acknowledgments

Several people who assisted me in this project deserve thanks. The staff at Temple University Press have been both professional and patient in guiding me through the publication process. I am grateful for their initial interest and generous support.

As a graduate student at the University of Wisconsin — Madison, I especially benefited from the guidance of three individuals. Joel Grossman enhanced my appreciation of public law, supported me in countless ways, and demanded a proper level of scholarship. Booth Fowler's influence extends beyond critiquing a manuscript. His intellect, generosity, enthusiasm, and friendship enrich both my work and faith. Donald Downs oversaw the original manuscript with extraordinary patience and encouragement. He is a first-rate scholar, a top-notch instructor, and a valued friend.

I dedicate this book to two remarkable women: my grandmother and my wife. I treasure the love, goodness, and generosity of Jessie Wheeler, my grandmother. During the last years of her life she prayed that I would receive my Ph.D., get married, and become a father. I did. Finally, through her love, patience, and insistence, Sheryl

Ann Lane helped me avoid being consumed or paralyzed by this project. (Our daughters, Anna and Sarah, gleefully assisted her in this effort.) She enriches my life in wondrous ways, and it was no accident that we met in church.

Beyond the Schoolhouse Gate

One

Pursuing Excellence and Order

First Amendment rights, applied in light of the special characteristics of the school environment, are available to teachers and students.

Tinker v. Des Moines Independent Community School District

To protest their nation's involvement in the Vietnam War, three Des Moines, Iowa, students arrived at school in December 1965 wearing black armbands. School officials promptly suspended them for violating a recently adopted policy prohibiting such actions. The United States Supreme Court, in a landmark 1969 case, held that the suspensions violated the First Amendment.[1]

During a pep rally at an Arkansas high school in 1968, twenty-nine black students walked out of the gymnasium to protest the playing of "Dixie." They were subsequently suspended by school officials, and the students brought action charging that the suspensions violated their First Amendment rights. A United States court of appeals upheld the suspensions in 1972, declaring that First Amendment rights may be infringed upon by reasonable regulations necessary for maintaining orderly conduct during school sessions.[2]

In 1986, outside a fast-food restaurant in Maine, a high school student directed a vulgar gesture at one of his teachers. Upon receiving a ten-day suspension, the student sought First Amendment protection for his actions. In 1986, a United States district court found no sufficient connection between the student's gesture and the proper and orderly operation of the school's activities and held the suspension to be unconstitutional.[3]

These three incidents illustrate the broad range of litigation that has taken place concerning the First Amendment rights of public school students. In the first case, students were engaged in symbolic political expression. In the second incident, the student protest occurred in an atmosphere of racial strife. And in the third incident, the student's vulgar gesture demonstrates, at the very least, interpersonal conflict between student and teacher. These occurrences, and the subsequent court rulings, raise important questions and concerns. On what grounds, if any, do public school students merit First Amendment protection? What should the scope and strength of this protection be? What values and interests regarding public schooling should serve to limit student free speech?

Such questions deserve thoughtful analysis, for extending First Amendment rights to public school students forces us to examine the aims of public education, the changing legal status of children, and the values underlying freedom of expression. To do this, we must also consider the proper role of the federal courts in local school governance. Constructing First Amendment speech protection for students requires that we construct both a framework for thinking about student free speech and specific guidelines for conferring such protection upon public school students.

Concern about the state of public education in the United States comes from many corners. Liberals assail schools for not doing a better job of ameliorating social and economic inequalities based upon race, class, gender, religion, and ethnicity. Conservatives blame schools for our nation's economic decline, as well as for social decay. Radicals often dismiss education as a totally dependent capitalist institution, incapable of restructuring American society.[4] Mainstream critics bemoan both dismal academic performance and unruly student behavior. Demands for educational reform cut across social, economic, and political divisions in our society, and public schools, perhaps as never before, feel pressure both to improve academic performance and to establish and maintain classroom order. These dual pursuits — of academic excellence and classroom order — often inflame conflicts between students and school officials, which in turn generate litigation regarding the constitutional rights of students. The relationship between the dual pursuits and constitutional litigation warrants detailed discussion.

The Pursuit of Excellence

If an unfriendly foreign power had attempted to impose on America the mediocre educational performance that exists today, we might well have viewed it as an act of war. As it stands, we have allowed this to happen to ourselves. We have even squandered the gains in student achievement made in the wake of the Sputnik challenge. Moreover, we have dismantled essential support systems which helped make those gains possible.

> We have, in effect, been committing an act of unthinking, uni-
> lateral educational disarmament.[5]

Throughout the 1980s, a sense of crisis regarding American public education made educational reform a salient topic on the political agenda.[6] An array of national reports warned that our public schools were inadequately educating the nation's youth.[7] While these national reports differed in their focus, findings, and recommendations, they shared a common belief that public schools play a crucial role in the nation's social and economic development, that increased leadership and accountability were needed, and that the quality of teachers had to be enhanced.[8]

In 1984, a federally sponsored report, A Nation at Risk, received considerable notoriety. The report warned that our public schools were suffering from increasing mediocrity in the quality of teachers, the academic skills of students, and the content of school curriculum.[9] High school standardized tests and college entrance exams revealed an overall decline in academic performance. The amount of homework assigned had decreased. American students were spending considerably less time in school, both in hours per day and days per year, than were students in most other industrialized nations. The amount of time devoted to the study of mathematics and science was one-third what students in Europe and Japan were spending. Finally, both the private sector and the nation's armed services were devoting millions of dollars each year to remedial training and education programs.[10]

The report concluded that this dismal state of public education was jeopardizing U.S. economic prowess in the global economy.[11] The report declared that educational reform was imperative and that the aim of such reform ought to be "excellence."[12] It recommended a greater role for the federal government, increased financial support from state and local governments, enforcement of rigorous attendance and discipline policies, and the establishment of concrete standards regarding teaching, curriculum, and student performance. In sum, *A Nation at Risk* raised educational reform to a prominent place on the public policy agenda of the 1980s. In noting the tenth anniversary of the report, Edward Fiske assessed its importance:

> It is difficult to overstate the impact of *A Nation at Risk* through the rest of the 1980s. Its depiction of the dismal state of American public education inspired a national school reform movement that was the first since the launching of Sputnik by the Soviet Union in 1957, and the largest ever. Within a year or so of the appearance of the report, every state legislature and statewide board of education had enacted some sort of school improvement program — most of them in line with the steps recommended by the commission.[13]

Thus, the pursuit of academic excellence took center stage in the debate over reforming American public schools.[14]

The Pursuit of Order

> During school hours a teacher is authorized to subject youngsters to regulation of the minutest details. A school-teacher's control approaches total power. Unless students comply, unless they show up at a particular school, attend a particular class, behave in particular ways, complete particular tasks, and reach a particular level of skill at doing them, then teachers may reduce their grades, humiliate them, extend their school day, withhold their diplomas, and, in the last resort, initiate criminal proceedings against them and their parents for attempting to flee the school-house. . . . Students live under the threats of teachers, and teachers are authorized to bring those threats to bear on any wayward defiance of their regime.[15]

Like other national reports, *A Nation at Risk* paid cursory attention to disciplinary concerns. In this it differed from students, parents, educators, and the general public.[16]

Recognizing the necessity and difficulty of controlling the behavior of students in the classroom, teachers expend considerable effort to minimize disruptive behavior. Teacher-training manuals often stress classroom management techniques and behavior modification strategies.[17] Many teachers use positive reinforcement, whether praise or more tangible rewards[18] or, occasionally, coercive measures, such as the use of psychostimulant drugs for extremely disruptive students.[19] In addition, regulating student behavior remains a prominent institutional feature of public schools.[20] Rules about fighting, littering, insubordination, bomb threats, physical assault, playground etiquette, school bus conduct, possession of alcohol and other drugs, and neglecting to return required forms are standard fare. However necessary and reasonable, they illustrate the extraordinary effort put forth to control student behavior.

Besides the everyday concerns of classroom behavior and violation of school rules, the criminal conduct of students is receiving increasing public attention.[21] Each year, tens of thousands of teachers are assaulted in our schools.[22] School vandalism annually costs taxpayers hundreds of millions of dollars.[23] Thefts and assaults on students number in the hundreds of thousands each year.[24] Although experts disagree over the proper conclusions to be drawn from the statistical evidence about crime in the schools, public concern remains understandably high.

Public concern about school crime and classroom order increases the pressure on school officials to control students.[25] For example, school authorities are pressured to combat the use of illegal drugs among students. In 1986, a Gallup poll found that the public's greatest concern about the public schools was the use of drugs.[26] Not surprisingly, in 1987 United States Attorney General Edwin Meese declared that few aspects of the drug problem were more frightening and troublesome than the presence of drugs in the schools,[27] and Secretary of Education William Bennett exhorted school officials to establish and maintain drug-free schools:

> Schools are uniquely situated to be part of the solution to student drug use. Children spend much of their time in school. Furthermore, schools, along with families and religious institutions, are major influences in transmitting ideals and standards of right and wrong. Thus, although the problems of drug use extend far beyond the schools, it is critical that our offensive on drugs centers in the schools.[28]

Since the 1960s, public opinion polls have consistently found that the public sees school discipline as a major problem confronting the public schools.[29] That concern has escalated, now that illegal drugs and violent crime have joined more conventional student mischief as common student activities.

Paradoxical Pursuits

The pursuit of excellence has profound consequences for the pursuit of order. American educators typically share a fundamental pedagogical premise: classroom order is essential to the educational enterprise. In other words, without order, there can be no learning. Historically, classroom order has meant that students should be passive, silent, and obedient. Significantly, the Supreme Court has shared this pedagogical claim:

> The primary duty of school officials and teachers, as the Court states, is the education and training of young people. A State has a compelling interest in assuring that the schools meet this responsibility. Without first establishing discipline and maintaining order, teachers cannot begin to educate their students.[30]

This linkage between order and learning helps us understand the extraordinary effort educators make toward establishing and maintaining order. Learning corresponds with order in a reciprocal fashion, for as learning increases, disorder decreases; conversely, as classroom order increases, so does learning.[31] Those who are not learning, who are not engaged in the educational enterprise, are more likely to disrupt the educational order and be disciplined for it.[32]

A paradoxical tension between learning and order reveals itself in various ways.[33] Disciplinary punishment, such as suspension and expulsion, impairs learning since the punished students are off educational task. Of course, the suspension of disruptive students may well facilitate the learning of other students, but unnecessary discipline may exacerbate the educational deficiencies of those who are already struggling academically.

Similarly, if students perceive school discipline to be unfair, excessive, and arbitrary, they may be more likely to resist and resent school officials. This adversarial stance is at odds with a positive learning environment. For this reason, William Muir argues that school discipline is especially problematic, for the teacher's authority over student conduct rests upon coercion.[34] Although coercive measures may produce immediate results in changing disorderly behavior, they also run the risk of undermining the moral authority of teachers. The result is a highly charged adversarial relationship between students and teachers that undermines the cooperation needed in the classroom, since it remains difficult, if not impossible, to coerce learning.

In addition, pursuing order costs time and money that could be devoted to other educational tasks, creating a tension with academic excellence. Schools now spend thousands of dollars on security officers, the cost of school vandalism runs into the tens of millions of dollars each year, and efforts to test students for drugs and alcohol drain precious school resources. Altogether, such get-tough measures, however necessary, strain the limited resources of public schools. Therefore, such measures may be ineffective, or even counterproductive, in the context of the broader educational mission. Conversely, pursuing academic excellence may have a profound impact on classroom order. For example, proponents of educational excellence often advocate legalistic and bureaucratic measures, such as standardized testing of students, which invariably further the quest for classroom order.[35] The relationship between bureaucratization and order links the dual pursuits of academic achievement and classroom order. Historically, as public schools became increasingly bureaucratized throughout the twentieth century, the pursuit of order accelerated. As David Kirp points out, establishing institutional order is an endemic feature of bureaucratic organizations, for it promotes both efficiency and hierarchical arrangements, thereby serving key bureaucratic norms:

> In schools, as in other organizations, ways of solving recurrent issues invariably become transformed into standard operating procedures. These rules "permit stable expectations to be formed by each member of the group as to the behavior of the other members under specified conditions," and thus allow the organization to run smoothly. They enable administrators to impose some checks upon the authority exercised by teachers, and they permit teachers to maintain stable relationships with students, avoiding accusations of favoritism or claims that they have let a particular child "get away with something."[36]

Thus, bureaucratic and legalistic educational reforms aimed at academic excellence will invariably exacerbate the institutional quest for order.

The dual pursuits of academic excellence and classroom order are paradoxically intertwined. Achieving order remains a constant struggle for school officials, and punishing students invariably saps their time, energy, and resources. Thus, the pursuit of order may hinder the pursuit of academic excellence, resulting in a catch-22 dilemma. Education requires order, but the excessive pursuit of order thwarts learning, resulting in reduced order and learning in many schools. This paradoxical relationship fuels the frustration of students, teachers, parents, and administrators, and it contributes to conflicts over the disciplinary authority of school officials.

Classroom Conflicts

Punishing students remains a crucial element of the pursuit of order. Although the pedagogical value of punishment is hotly debated, the historical relationship between punishment and U.S. public education is well established.[37] For more than two centuries, school officials in the United States have pursued classroom order by punishing students. Carl Kaestle, a noted educational historian, finds the relationship between public schooling and instilling moral discipline in students firmly established by the early nineteenth century.[38] The legal historian Lawrence Friedman, in fact, believes that discipline was at the core of public schooling throughout the nineteenth century.[39] Furthermore, punishment was frequently disproportionate to student behavior. Misbehaviors were rarely criminal or violent; instead, students were often punished for tardiness, profanity, "immorality," hyperactivity, and short attention span. Yet the punishments included flogging, shackling, humiliation, time in the portable pillory, and the infamous "log" described by David Sabatino:

> The Log was prescribed for students with short attention spans. Those who fidgeted and squirmed had a cord slipped over their heads and a 6-pound log was balanced on each individual's shoulders. The slightest motion one way or the other and the equilibrium was lost, with the log putting a dead weight on the neck.[40]

Today, school officials frequently discipline students via expulsions, suspensions, and corporal punishment.[41] A conservative estimate is that 9 percent of the entire student body is suspended during the school year.[42] Corporal punishment remains commonplace, according to a survey conducted by the U.S. Office of Civil Rights.[43] Indeed, Stanley Rothstein describes schools as disciplinary structures rather than educational institutions:

> Since the end of the 19th century, the life of urban schooling continues to manifest itself in the disciplinary structures associated with huge, bureaucratic organizations — condemning new generations to an education obsessed with selection, confinement, and discipline, resisting, with the aid of powerful forces in society, all calls for a more humane, more scientific, more success-oriented training.[44]

Similarly, Richard Merelman argues that the organizational structure of schools makes the problem of order especially acute because they bring together a large, heterogeneous body of emotionally immature but physically active adolescents.[45]

The pervasive, often aggressive penchant for student discipline and classroom order is understandable, if not always prudent. Indeed, pupils who engage in unruly, disruptive, and dangerous behavior warrant disciplinary action. Some students seek attention by showing off or by snapping their fingers. Others conduct themselves in a rude, offensive manner and disrupt the class by arriving late, playing practical jokes, or taking the possessions of others. And, as mentioned earlier, many students engage in criminal conduct, such as theft, assault, or vandalism.[46] Accordingly, schools establish extensive rules and regulations, and, not surprisingly, students often feel the force of disciplinary action.

Conflicts between students and educators regarding student conduct and official punishment occasionally result in litigation. For example, school officials are frequently taken to task over such controversial, get-tough measures as drug testing, searching students and property, banning "beepers," and restricting gang-associated dress.[47] Not surprisingly, such litigation raises important constitutional issues. Students have demanded First Amendment protection of speech, press, and expression.[48] The federal courts have handed down numerous decisions regarding Fourth Amendment challenges to searches conducted on school grounds.[49] Parents have unsuccessfully argued that corporal punishment violates the Eighth Amendment ban on cruel and unusual punishment.[50] Fourteenth Amendment due process challenges have also been brought before the federal courts.[51] Classroom conflicts between students and school officials encompass a broad spectrum of constitutional issues.

The political saliency of educational reform exacerbates the dual pursuits of academic excellence and classroom order. These pursuits occur amid demands for the extension of constitutional rights to students and a growing concern about mediocre academic performance, illicit drugs, gang violence, teenage pregnancy, and other problems facing our nation's youth.[52] Increasingly, disputes that begin in the classroom compel the federal courts to consider whether public school students enjoy constitutional protection.

This inquiry examines the extent to which the First Amendment ought to protect student speech. This focus on free speech recognizes the historical importance of First Amendment disputes in forging constitutional rights for students. In an important 1969 ruling, the United States Supreme Court recognized public school students as independent "constitutional persons," and for more than twenty years the lower courts have decided scores of cases pertaining to student expression.[53]

Along with the historical importance of First Amendment cases, a detailed inquiry into student free speech acknowledges the elevated status of the First Amendment, which enjoys a prominent place in constitutional doctrine. Accordingly, an inquiry into the First Amendment rights of students provides insight into key issues and concerns pertaining to the panorama of their constitutional rights. Finally, focusing on the First Amendment illuminates four related discussions regarding First Amendment doctrine, the aims of public schooling, the role of the judiciary in school governance, and the legal status of children.

Conclusion

Three fields of scholarship inform this examination and discussion of student free speech. The public education literature typically provides a macrolevel analysis of social forces, public pressures, and institutional structures.[54] The constitutional rights of students receive little attention. When addressed, they are typically a footnote to a broader concern, such as school reform or the expansion of judicial power.[55]

The children's rights literature frequently debates universal rights conferred at birth, but it does not devote enough attention to the constitutional rights of children.[56] The polemical character of this literature presents children's rights as part of an expansive radical agenda. Hence, the liberation of children is inextricably linked with the liberation of all.[57]

The free speech literature suffers from the narrow scope and focus of the authors. This narrowness applies to both the limited number of court cases discussed (often only one Supreme Court decision) and the range of disputes addressed.[58] For example, some commentators address only the removal of library books or the censorship of school-sponsored newspapers.[59] Others focus on a single issue, such as the public-forum analysis employed by the Court.[60] While the Supreme Court understandably receives considerable scrutiny, lower federal court decisions warrant greater attention, since the broad range of disputes involved demonstrates the complexity of forging First Amendment protection for public school students.

In order to redress these shortcomings, this inquiry utilizes lower federal court decisions as well as those of the Supreme Court. In addition, three areas of disputes are examined, illuminating the complexity of student free speech; this discussion is descriptive, analytical, and normative. The descriptive component discusses the emergence of children's rights, along with contemporary constitutional doctrine. The analytical component examines both the legal reasoning employed by the courts and the controversies regarding student free speech. Finally, the normative component considers the legal status of children, the proper parameters of the First Amendment, and the role of the courts in school governance and educational policy making.

This synthesis, I hope, offers a persuasive argument that provides a framework for thinking about student free speech, along with specific guidelines for granting students First Amendment protection. The analysis and argument reflect the fact that free-speech disputes differ in significant ways, that children require a healthy mix of protection and autonomy, and that the inculcative function — the transmission of values — plays a vital role in public schooling. This contribution to the debate regarding the First Amendment rights of students underscores the claim that strongly held positions need not be extreme.

Two

The Emergence of Children's Rights

When we say of children's needs, as of their

virtues, that they belong only to children, we

make them seem trivial, we invalidate them.

What is more important, we insure that they

will not be met. For no amount of

sentimentalizing or preaching will make a

society provide for its young people a better

quality of life than it provides for its adults.

We fool ourselves if we think ways can be

found to give children what all the rest of us

so sorely lack.

John Holt, *The Children's Rights Movement*

To understand the difficulty of forging constitutional rights for adolescents, we must appreciate the tension between social integration and individual autonomy. As a semiautonomous stage of development, adolescence is both a period in itself and a transitional time of trial and error.[1] Franklin Zimring notes the disjuncture between the static legal position of adolescents and the contours of this stage:

> As a period of semi-autonomy, it places special burdens on legal reasoning and public choice. As a transition to adulthood, it demands a future orientation in public policy. How we grow up is an important determinant of what kinds of adults we grow up to be. . . . [A]dolescence requires a peculiar mix of liberty and order that is anything but simple to achieve.[2]

Examining the changing legal status of children helps us understand the emergence of independent constitutional rights for public school students.

Colonial America: Chattel Status

From colonial times until late in the nineteenth century, the legal status of children was analogous to chattel property. They were controlled either by parents or by those supervising their apprenticeship. The indenture and binding out of children, along with involuntary apprenticeship, were an integral part of colonial life.[3] "Both family and government had a part in keeping everyone constructively employed. It was the child's duty to work, the father's legal obligation to prepare him for a useful occupation, and the responsibility of the magistrates to provide obligation work for the poor and punish the idle."[4] The survival of the new settlements required child labor, and children often assumed adult economic roles at an early age, although they had little legal control over earnings.[5]

In addition, children were subjected to the same criminal procedures and punishments as adults.[6] At least on paper, they could face extraordinary criminal sanctions; some states, for example, permitted the imposition of the death penalty for incorrigible, rebellious behavior.[7] In practice, children received fines and public whippings for cursing at their parents or masters. Corporal punishment was widespread, and it was inflicted upon children who were unduly idle.[8] Reflecting attitudes that shaped the legal status of colonial children, the legislature of Massachusetts, the General Court, proclaimed a "Day of humiliation" to address "the great ignorance and inclination of the rising generation to vanity, profaneness, and disobedience."[9] From an early age, children were warned that idleness undermined the social order and destroyed young souls.[10] Economic necessity justified child labor, and religion sanctified it.

Legally recognized emancipation emerged during the 1800s, but special legal rights for children were almost nonexistent.[11] No legal distinction existed among neglected, delinquent, and runaway children. Minors convicted of serious crimes were subjected to adult punishments, and those convicted of lesser offenses, such as stealing, gambling, or vandalism, were typically sent to community asylums or homes. Prior to the reform era of the late nineteenth century, no special facilities existed for the care of youths in trouble with the law; nor were there separate laws or courts to control their behavior.[12]

The Progressive Era: Emergence of Parens Patriae Doctrine

From 1870 to 1920, a parens patriae doctrine, giving legal authority to the state to control and supervise children, displaced their chattel legal status.[13] This development corresponded with the social upheaval resulting from the urbanization and industrialization of the United States.[14] With adults increasingly experiencing uncertainty, dislocation, and alienation, intergenerational roles and responsibilities were reallocated.[15]

The parens patriae doctrine both shaped and reflected profound changes in public policy, familial relations, parental authority, and the lives of children. It rests upon three postulates. First, since childhood is a period of dependency and risk, supervision is essential for survival. Second, while the family is of primary importance, the state may justifiably intervene when the family fails. Finally, the interests of a child-at-risk ought to be decided by public officials.[16]

In addition, this doctrine underpinned the three main areas of reform implemented during this period: compulsory-education laws, restriction of child labor, and the creation of a juvenile justice system.[17] For the Progressive child reformers, no matter what the cause, no matter who was at fault, state power could be invoked to save children.[18] Through the transfer of broad discretionary power to the state, children became, in effect, a newly regulated industry.

Progressive reformers viewed young people as being intrinsically good. Children misbehaved not because of some innate sinfulness but because social institutions corrupted them. Accordingly, the perfecting of the nation's innocent youth was possible only if corrupt institutions were swept away and a proper environment for children was established.[19] Because of their innate innocence, girls and boys were seen as especially vulnerable to abuse, corruption, and exploitation. For Progressives, children were tragically exploited in the workplace and frequently abused and neglected at home, and their spiritual, emotional, and physical well-being were endangered by their parents, other adults, and various socioeconomic forces and institutions. In addition, because children tend to see their desires and needs as synonymous, youngsters were too immature to make critical decisions about their own welfare. Such immaturity required that adult proxies make important decisions for them.

This Progressive view of children as vulnerable and immature corresponded with the reformers' assessment of family life. The Progressive child savers saw families as the primary culprits in the corruption and victimization of children; whether unwittingly or deliberately, parents created social misfits, potential criminals, emotional cripples, and juvenile delinquents. Thus, families who did not fulfill their important social functions in child rearing were seen as obstacles to social progress. According to Christopher Lasch, reformers diagnosed these families as "sick," thereby justifying the state in taking over their social functions:

> In order to justify their appropriation of parental functions, the "helping professions" in their formative period — roughly from 1900 to 1930 — appealed many times to the analogy of preventive medicine and public health. Educators, psychiatrists, social workers, and penologists, saw themselves as doctors to a sick society, and they demanded the broadest possible delegation of medical authority in order to heal it.[20]

The Progressive reforms facilitated adult supervision of children by transferring boys and girls from the workplace to public schools. Removing children from much of the workforce required the reformers to identify the evils of child labor.[21] The Progressives attacked this practice for restricting the moral, physical, spiritual, and emotional development of children. Furthermore, they argued that

child labor augured ill for the nation's future, for it endangered economic development and accelerated the disintegration of the family.

While delineating the evils of child labor, the reformers simultaneously defended compulsory education. It would combat widespread illiteracy and ignorance and provide some self-protection for
society, since the education of one's children was both an individual
duty to the child and a collective duty to society.[22] The reformers
expected compulsory education to compensate for the failings of
parents, particularly immigrants.[23]

Transferring children from the workforce to the classroom, however, did not sufficiently address the needs and problems associated with "children-at-risk," who were abused, troubled, neglected,
delinquent, or criminal. Progressive reformers considered these
young people "salvageable" as well, and their salvation required
both proper treatment and supervision. The child-saving movement,
then, corresponded with the rapid increase in helping professionals
ready and willing to "treat" children and families. These professionals established standards for children's welfare, resulting in a
proliferation of foster homes, orphan asylums, and other institutions for dependent youngsters, all supervised by the state.

Perhaps the crowning achievement of the Progressive child reformers was the establishment of the juvenile courts. Illinois set up
the first such system in 1899, and all but three states had followed its
lead by 1917.[24] Juvenile courts represented the Progressive marriage
of supervision and treatment for troubled children.[25] As Christopher
Lasch explains:

> The reform of juvenile justice in the progressive period best ex-
> emplifies the connections between therapeutic conceptions of
> society, the rise of social pathology as a profession, and the ap-
> propriation of familial functions by agencies of socialized re-
> production. The juvenile court movement rested on the belief
> that juvenile delinquency originated in deformed homes. Ac-

cordingly, the juvenile delinquent was to be treated not as a criminal but as a victim of circumstances.[26]

From the beginning, juvenile court judges proclaimed their commitment to rehabilitation rather than punishment,[27] reflecting faith and optimism that they could change the behavior of wayward children.[28]

These child reforms were the centerpiece of a broader Progressive agenda that sought to expand state authority in response to the perceived excesses of capitalism and the social ills created by immigration and urbanization.[29] Progressive reformers hoped that early intervention in child rearing would temper selfish individualism.[30] They also sought to regulate anarchic business conditions, promote cooperation between capitalists and workers, and reduce economic and social inequality through taxation and educational reform. The child reforms served the interests of the social workers and professionals who constituted the core of the Progressive movement.[31] Witness the rhetoric of Felix Adler, a professor of political and social ethics at Columbia University, founder of the Ethical Culture Society, and chairman of the National Child Labor Committee, in a speech he delivered at the first annual meeting of the last-named group in 1905.

> The emancipation of childhood from economic servitude is a social reform of the first magnitude. . . . Because if it comes to be an understood thing that a certain sacredness "doth hedge around" a child, that a child is industrially taboo, that to violate its rights is to touch profanely a holy thing, that it has a soul which must not be blighted for the prospect of mere gain; if this be once generally conceded with regard to the child, the same essential reasoning will be found to apply also to the adult workers; they, too, will not be looked upon as mere commodities, as mere instruments for the accumulation of riches. . . . I have great hopes for the adjustment of our labor difficulties on a higher plane, if once we can gain the initial vic-

tory of inculcating regard for the higher human nature that is present potentially in the child.[32]

Progressives Reconsidered

There are conflicting interpretations of the motives and intentions of the reformers.[33] The traditional view assigns to them the highest of motives, concluding that they sincerely wished to serve the best interests of children. Here, the reformers were profoundly disturbed by the standard application of adult procedures and punishments to youthful offenders, and they believed that rather than inflicting harsh punishment the state ought to provide care and assistance for such children.[34]

Revisionists, however, maintain that the reformers pursued the self-serving professional and political interests of the middle and upper classes. For example, not all of the arguments given for restricting child labor merit applause. A common view among southern child labor reformers pertained to the region's racial balance:

> [T]he children who are at work in the southern cotton mills are from the white working class of the South; and this terrible situation stares the South in the face that, whereas the children of the white working people of the South are going to the mill and to decay, the negro children are going to school and improvement. I am glad to see the negro children going to school, but it is enough to wring the heart to think that day by day you are permitting a system to go on which is steadily weakening the white race for the future and steadily strengthening the black race for the future.[35]

Similarly, revisionists argue that the actual operation of the juvenile courts was severe and impersonal rather than humane and compassionate.[36]

Revisionists and traditionalists would agree, however, that Progressive reforms dramatically transformed the legal position of children. Status offenses like violating curfew, truancy, and the consumption of alcohol proliferated, so that actions perfectly acceptable for adults were criminal if committed by minors. Other age-based exclusions, such as curtailment of employment opportunities, received legal sanction as well.

The legal status of children also entailed inescapable custody. The state assigned custody of those removed from their parents to another family or a particular institution, or simply made them wards of the state. Juvenile courts typically made such decisions; as Charles Silberman explains, they were not necessarily in the best interests of children:

> The euphemistic language and medical metaphors of "the juvenile court philosophy" persuade judges of their own benevolence, blinding them to the havoc they sometimes wreak in children's lives. "If you see a man approaching with the obvious intent of doing you good," Thoreau warned, "you should run for your life." But children usually are not in a position to run; and if they do, their running itself becomes a basis for further intervention by the court.[37]

The result was a curious hybrid legal status, in which the delinquent (or criminal) child was thought of more as a patient than as a criminal. The judge became part physician, and proceedings brought against juvenile delinquents were considered to be more civil than criminal.[38] According to Silberman, this hybrid status too frequently resulted in irrational punishment. He found juvenile court judges to be prisoners of their own rhetoric, spending the bulk of their time on young people charged with status offenses (so-called because it is their status as minors that makes the acts illegal) rather than dealing with those juveniles who commit serious crimes.[39]

Furthermore, this legal status reflected the ambivalence of public policy toward children.[40] There was conflict between the goals of nurturing and protecting the young against older members of society and protecting society against the misbehaving young.[41] This ambivalence created juvenile courts in which, according to a 1967 Supreme Court ruling, the child receives the worst of both worlds, getting neither the protections accorded to adults nor the solicitous care and regenerative treatment postulated for children.[42] Thus, the legal status of children established during the Progressive era denied them choice, autonomy, and self-determination. It reflected growing distrust of parental authority, and it showed confidence in educators, government, and professional social workers. These battles over the legal status of children focused upon custody, and they were not merely (or even primarily) a struggle between children and adults; they involved, rather, adults competing for authority over the nation's youth.

Child Liberators: The Quest for Autonomy

The parens patriae doctrine, along with the reforms of the Progressive era, shaped the legal status of children until the late 1960s. Youngsters enjoyed few independent legal rights, and the state held unfettered authority to intervene in their lives. However, amid the social and political upheaval of the 1960s, a vigorous, if somewhat eclectic, campaign to liberate children emerged.

Today's debate over the legal status of children reflects a challenge to the achievements of the Progressive era. Since the 1960s, activists have sought to provide children with the legal opportunity to determine life's critical decisions, thereby "liberating" them from virtually all forms of adult authority and supervision.[43]

Self-declared child liberators, displeased with the legal status of young people, argue that children should enjoy substantial autonomy.[44] They claim that youngsters are victims of neglect, violence, and oppression and that virtually all social institutions are the culprits, including those charged with the care and supervision of children.[45] For example, the liberators portray schools as rigid, repressive institutions that preserve the social order by inculcating conformity and passivity.[46] They condemn schools for reinforcing racial, social, and economic inequality, and they assail public educators for practicing a stifling pedagogy.[47] Not surprisingly, they want to liberate children from coercive school authority that thwarts self-determination and reinforces social stratification.[48] Along with this scathing critique of public schooling, liberators offer alternative visions of the educational mission. In 1968, George Leonard offered a representative view of a "liberating" education:

> If education in the coming age is to be not just a part of life, but the main purpose of life, then education's purpose will, at last, be viewed as central. What, then, is the purpose, the goal of education? A large part of the answer may well be what men of this civilization have longest feared and most desired: the achievement of moments of ecstasy. Not fun, not simply pleasure, as in the equation of Bentham and Mill, not the libido pleasure of Freud, but ecstasy, ananda, the ultimate delight.[49]

Thus, educational ecstasy becomes an antidote for oppressive schools obsessed with quantifying academic achievement and restricting student behavior.

Child liberators find victimization far beyond the schoolyard. Children, mired at the bottom of familial hierarchy, are often abused and neglected within the family unit. Flawed public policies and expenditures allow millions of girls and boys to live in poverty. Children feel the weight of cyclical "get tough" measures aimed at controlling their conduct. The private sector victimizes youngsters by inculcating an insatiable consumerist ethic and by stressing their role in a market economy. Even when liberators begrudgingly acknowledge that conditions have improved for millions of children over the years, they assail the motives underlying such gains:

> The conditions under which children are raised have improved over the course of time — and children's standards of living

may even have risen more rapidly than that of people in general. However, such "progress" needs to be examined closely to see if it represents a genuine concern for children as human beings or merely an interest in children as future participants in the socioeconomy.[50]

Child liberators paint a grim picture of childhood—a market economy exploits children by providing low wages, and the political system demonstrates indifference and hostility toward them while hypocritically declaring grave concern for the plight of our nation's youth. The liberators note that many young people experience stress, despair, and alienation, resulting in high levels of abuse of alcohol and other drugs and a disturbingly high rate of teenage suicide. In sum, they argue that the nation's social and economic ills fall especially hard upon children.

Consistent with this grim portrait of U.S. society, child liberators offer a devastating critique of both the motives and accomplishments of the Progressive child reformers. They argue that the agencies and institutions established by the reformers have performed dismally, contributing significantly to the oppression and victimization of children. Furthermore, they challenge the premises underpinning the Progressive reforms, as well as the true motives and intentions of the child savers.

Andrew Platt's influential critique of the juvenile justice system illustrates a revisionist assessment of the Progressive reforms. Platt gives four reasons why child savers should not be considered humanists or libertarians.[51] First, rather than ushering in a new system of justice, the reforms furthered traditional policies informally developed during the nineteenth century. Second, by assuming the dependence of adolescents, the Progressives established a juvenile court system to punish the premature independence and unacceptable behavior of young people. Third, the child savers' attitudes toward children-at-risk were largely romantic and paternalistic, though their efforts were backed up by force. Hence, they were mistakenly confident that a benevolent government could determine and serve the interests of troubled children. Finally, their correctional programs required longer terms of imprisonment, long hours of labor and militaristic discipline, and the inculcation of middle-class values and lower-class skills.[52] Together, Platt and other revisionists portray the Progressive child reformers as a mixture of deceptive, misguided, insincere, and hypocritical citizens responsible for oppressing and victimizing subsequent generations of children.[53]

Although they offer a harsh critique of the Progressive child reforms, the liberators fail to provide a clear vision of what children's lives ought to be like. To some extent, they suggest that boys and girls are more mature, more independent, and less vulnerable than child savers contend. They minimize the differences between children and adults by stressing youngsters' capacity for self-determination. They remain focused on the liberation of children rather than on providing an alternative vision of children's lives. Richard Farson, a prominent liberator, explains:

> To the question of what we really know about the potentialities of children, the answer will have to be that we do not know what children can do when they are at their best because we have not created the conditions necessary to elicit superior behavior. Indeed, in our society, it is virtually impossible to create such conditions. Until we develop a new appreciation for their rights and a new respect for their potential, we cannot know children.[54]

As was the case with the Progressive reformers, child liberators pursue a broad social agenda. They represent one strand of a larger radical movement that challenged authority in all its forms during the 1960s and 1970s.[55] Their critique of childhood is often part of a broader attack upon prevailing social norms and values. For many of them, the nation's primary social institutions are unremittingly racist, exclusive, bureaucratic, and undemocratic.[56] Accordingly, the liberation of children becomes part of a broader effort to restructure our socioeconomy:

> Exploitation of children can only be brought to an end in a socioeconomy in which the development of the individual is the highest social purpose and satisfaction of wants is understood to be possible in the absence of increased material production. It does not appear that such a socioeconomic system can evolve in the United States in the foreseeable future without major socioeconomic upheaval.[57]

Their demands for fundamental, often radical changes in our social, political, and economic institutions distinguish child liberators from contemporary child advocates.

Child Advocates: The Quest for Protection

Striking differences exist between child liberators and child advocates. Contemporary child savers (self-proclaimed child advocates) call for something less than a radical restructuring of society. They paint a less grim portrait of oppression and victimization, and they applaud the successes and achievements of the Progressive reformers. Advocates and liberators disagree over the role existing institutions play in the lives of children. The liberators view these as part of the problem, requiring either complete dismantling or fundamental transformation. The advocates, while acknowledging certain shortcomings of the status quo, nonetheless support the child-saving premises underpinning many institutions. They typically argue that existing problems result from a lack of will and commitment among adults to care for young people.[58] Here, public indifference becomes the culprit, rather than adults who pursue a hidden agenda or are driven by invidious motives. For child advocates, then, adults must find better ways to serve and protect children, rather than foolishly liberating them to fend for themselves.[59]

Not surprisingly, child advocates offer a different historical reading of the Progressive child-reform efforts. They deem several of
these to have largely succeeded, and they believe that Progressive
child savers significantly improved the lot of children, in spite of
acknowledged flaws.[60] Protecting, educating, and supervising children, especially those at risk, remain legitimate goals for advocates.
Like the Progressive reformers, advocates see children as especially
vulnerable to corruption, but nonetheless salvageable. They too call
for increasing the role of government, and express confidence in professional expertise. While contemporary advocates are more skeptical of institutions and bureaucracies than were the Progressive reformers, they consider the radical critics' attack upon the motives
and intent of their predecessors to be, in large measure, unfair and
unwarranted.[61]

Contemporary child advocates call for public policies that pursue
the best interests of children. Some assert that the primary function
of educators ought to be advocacy on behalf of young people;[62]
other child advocates demand higher wages, national health insur-
ance, more and better jobs for parents, and extensive training and
education for adults.[63] Together, this reform agenda reflects confidence in professional expertise and extensive intervention by benevolent adults. Like the Progressive child savers, child advocates aggressively pursue public and private funds. Witness the following
recommendations made by the 1970 White House Conference on
Children:

> [We] recommend that top priority be given to quickly estab-
> lishing a child advocacy agency financed by the Federal Gov-
> ernment and other sources with full ethnic, cultural, racial,
> and sexual representation. . . . [We] recommend that child-
> oriented environmental commissions be established at na-
> tional, state, and local levels to ensure that children's needs are
> not neglected by city planners, architects, building contractors,
> and others who influence how homes and neighborhoods are
> constructed.[64]

Like the Progressive reformers and contemporary liberators, child advocates are part of a broader social movement for women's rights, racial equality, and economic reform.[65]

Lee Teitelbaum offers an insightful assessment of the contemporary debate between child advocates and child liberators:

> [The] dispute concerning the legal and social position of youth is conducted by adversaries who commonly call themselves "advocates for the rights of children." Each group believes that how we treat children is of great importance and none could accept a label suggesting that it was in some way "anti-child." At the same time, these various advocates for children's rights propose very different places and programs for young people and start from very different socio-economic premises.[66]

Teitelbaum describes the differences among child advocates as part of a larger struggle between supporters of integrative and autonomous rights.

Integrative Rights

This position aims at extending provisions and protections necessary for the social integration of children into adult society. By emphasizing the needs of young people, rather than their desires, integrative rights stress the differences between children and adults. Such rights also presume boys and girls to be especially vulnerable and dependent. Proponents of integrative rights focus upon the duties of others, particularly the state, to provide for children. Integrative children's rights, then, are corollaries to adult duties.[67] Such rights require adult proxies to determine what youngsters need and to then deliver the necessary goods and services.[68]

Integrative rights do not end with the creation of a governmental duty. Rather, they presume the rightholder to have little choice in accepting provisions. For example, children have the right to an education, but it remains compulsory, because the emphasis is placed on the integration of children into society. Accordingly, the primary purpose of compulsory education is not to provide children with a shield against society; it is, rather, to require their exposure to knowledge, attitudes, and behavior patterns thought important by the society at large.[69] Similarly, rights to psychiatric care or psychological well-being seek to bring the recipient into the community rather than separating her from society.[70] As Teitelbaum points out, integrative rights are analogous to a railroad ticket.[71] Children are provided with transportation to a particular destination: adulthood. But they travel on a train from which they cannot freely depart, and they do not enjoy much say in how the train is operated.

Integrative rights found expression in a 1973 United Nations declaration of children's rights.[72] According to the United Nations, children in all countries are entitled to:

> special protection, opportunities, and facilities to enable them to develop in a healthy and normal manner, in freedom and dignity;
> social security, including adequate nutrition, housing, recreation, and medical services;
> love and understanding in an atmosphere of affection and security, in the care and under the responsibility of their parents whenever possible;
> free education and recreation and equal opportunity to develop their individual abilities;
> protection from all forms of neglect, cruelty, and exploitation; and
> protection from any form of racial, religious, or other discrimination, and an upbringing in a spirit of peace and universal brotherhood.

The securing of such rights, it is argued, ensures children of successful and meaningful integration into their particular community.

Autonomous Rights

This position provides a shield from social pressures and state authority.[73] By emphasizing autonomy and choice, these rights serve a distancing rather than an integrative function.[74] Not surprisingly, autonomous rights reflect a deep suspicion of authority, and they can be traced to John Stuart Mill's libertarian principle embracing the right to be let alone.

The noted child psychologist Richard Farson provides a contemporary bill of rights for children designed to secure self-determination.[75] The right to self-determination entails certain derivative rights:

> the right to alternative home environments;
> the right to responsive design;
> the right to information;
> the right to educate oneself;
> the right to freedom from physical punishment;
> the right to sexual freedom;
> the right to economic power;
> the right to political power; and
> the right to justice.

This proposed bill of rights appears absolute in scope, and it apparently applies to all children, since no specific age limit is proposed. For example, Farson argues that the right to sexual freedom extends not merely to sexual conduct, including incest, but to an absolute right to sex information:

> [T]he right to sex information would mean eliminating all forms of censorship which keep children ignorant about sex and giving them access to all of the information to which adults have access. Specifically, this would include books in libraries which, as we have seen, are arbitrarily and systematically kept out of the hands of children. Much to the discomfort

of adults, it would also include the right to enter stores and theaters where "adults only" films, magazines, and other sexual entertainment is presented. Pornography is neither the best nor one of the most common sources of sex information, but we must recognize it as an important source, even if we find it personally distasteful. Although the pictures of sex which one receives from pornography are at least as distorted as those from public school sex education, they can provide many answers which the child simply does not get from adults.[76]

Similarly, Farson argues that a child ought to enjoy coextensive economic power, including the right to receive credit, conduct financial negotiations, hold union membership, and determine conditions of employment.[77] Admittedly, his views are more extreme than those of other child liberators, but they should not be summarily dismissed as absurd or inconsequential, for he enjoyed an esteemed, if controversial, place in the liberation movement.[78]

The conflict between integrative and autonomous rights, of course, parallels the debate about protection and autonomy for children. In the United States, integrative rights found their most comprehensive expression in the Progressive child reforms[79] — compulsory education, child labor laws, and the juvenile court sought the social integration of children.[80] Teitelbaum explains:

> Rights of the kind described as "integrative" plainly imply nothing in the way of choice on the part of the rightholder; as applied to children, their principal thrust is in quite the other direction. Compulsory education and child labor laws were justified in great part by the desire to prevent children from becoming financially or socially independent before they were ready for that. Jurisdiction over "incorrigible" children likewise sought to deter premature assertions of freedom from control.[81]

By constructing a shield against state authority, autonomous rights are antithetical to Progressive ideals and principles. By emphasizing choice and self-determination, autonomous rights secure legally enforceable rights for children that are coextensive with those enjoyed by adults. Such rights challenge the Progressive justifications for status offenses, juvenile courts, compulsory education, and, perhaps, even child labor laws.[82]

Similarly, both views of rights inform the debate regarding the constitutional rights of children. Teitelbaum argues that integrative rights correspond with the long-standing American quest for equality, which reflects a wish to be like rather than different from others.[83] Accordingly, public entitlements, such as public education, are referred to as rights that ought to be equally available to all children, regardless of race, gender, religion, or disability.

However, autonomy rights correspond with those liberties and freedoms associated with the U.S. Bill of Rights. The view of rights as guarantees of autonomy lies at the origins of the federal Constitution. According to Teitelbaum, the fundamental principles of that document derive largely from the eighteenth-century views in which individual rights were considered natural, even antecedent to government. When the people adopted the Constitution, they retained their autonomy and individual liberties against the government, which was expected to protect those freedoms.[84]

Because child development theories, as well as constitutional doctrine, embrace both positions, we should be wary of discarding one view of rights in favor of the other. Teitelbaum elaborates:

> Neither theory is legally or socially inappropriate to children; indeed, both are explicitly incorporated within every view of proper child-rearing. On the one hand, it is expected that children will be acculturated; that is, they will learn cultural values in general and learn to conform their conduct to social rules in particular. They must, in short, become knowledgeable members of the community. At the same time, the end point of these processes is adulthood, when the child becomes a full citizen who must have developed a capacity for choice and autonomous action.[85]

Failure either to protect children or to deny them opportunities for self-determination entails grave consequences. In order to join the society in which she lives, a child must learn social rules and values. Conversely, a child growing up without the capacity for independent choice will be ill-equipped to become an active participant in a pluralistic, democratic society. Since this tension cannot be eliminated, it would be foolish to abandon either view of rights.[86] Instead, as Hillary Rodham notes, we should recognize three legitimate approaches to forging children's rights.[87] One, embraced by child liberators, makes the rights of young people coextensive with those of adults. Another approach, embodied in Supreme Court decisions, modifies adult rights. A third approach, typically taken by child advocates, seeks rights specially tailored for children. The challenge lies in reconciling these competing approaches.

Constitutional Rights: A Lower Threshold

In addressing children's rights, we must invariably consider the proper distance between adults' rights and those granted youngsters. Forging constitutional rights for children, therefore, requires a comparative approach: How similar should these rights be to those enjoyed by adults? The United States Supreme Court has properly concluded that children merit less constitutional protection than adults. This modified constitutional status of children reveals a tension between protection and autonomy, a theme that will be prominent in examining the First Amendment rights of public school students.

A limited examination of the constitutional rights of children outside the public school environment illuminates the Court's rationale for establishing a modified sphere of First Amendment protection for public school students. The constitutional status of children outside the educational setting reveals the interplay between protection and autonomy, and it thereby indirectly sheds light on the conflict between integrative and autonomous rights. The Supreme

Court decisions pertaining to sexuality and due process demonstrate both the Court's effort to tailor constitutional rights for children and the tension between protection and autonomy.

The present constitutional status of young people tries to strike a balance between not granting any constitutional rights to children and making such rights coextensive with those of adults. What is at issue, then, is determining a lower constitutional threshold for state authority over children. The United States Supreme Court established this lower threshold in *Prince v. Massachusetts*,[88] upholding a Massachusetts law prohibiting children from selling magazines, newspapers, and the like in a public place. (The statute applied to boys under the age of twelve and to girls under the age of eighteen.) The law also made it a criminal offense to furnish such goods to a child for sale in a public place. The guardian aunt of the children involved was prosecuted for enlisting them as street proselytizers for the family's religious faith. The Court weighed a substantial state interest in protecting the welfare of youngsters against the asserted individual interests of the aunt.[89] Accordingly, the Court noted that neither freedom of religion nor parental authority is absolute. In addition, it stated that the government, acting as parens patriae, may regulate the activities of children to a greater extent than it can those of adults, particularly in the case of public activities and in matters of employment.[90] The Court explained:

> A democratic society rests, for its continuance, upon the healthy, well-rounded growth of young people into full maturity as citizens, with all that implies. It may secure this against impending restraints and dangers, within a broad range of selection. Among evils most appropriate for such action are the crippling effects of child employment, more specifically in public places, and the possible harms arising from other activities subject to all the diverse influences of the street.[91]

Prince, then, signaled that parental authority was not without limits, and in the future the Court would balance the individual rights involved against the state's authority to impose necessary and reasonable restrictions in order to achieve some legitimate purpose.[92]

Sexuality

The Supreme Court decisions regarding sexuality and children's rights exhibit an effort to grant limited autonomy to minors, as well as permitting states broad protective powers. Broadly speaking, when the Court grants children constitutional protection in this area, their autonomy is expanded. Conversely, when the Court permits states to regulate children to a greater degree than is allowed for adults, powers of protection are broadened.

Certain sexuality rulings, congruent with *Prince,* establish a lower constitutional threshold. In a 1968 case, *Ginsberg v. New York,* the Supreme Court upheld a New York statute prohibiting the sale of pornographic material to minors.[93] Consistent with *Prince,* the court recognized a significant state interest in protecting the well-being of children, thereby allowing the state to prohibit the distribution of materials to minors that may not be barred from adults.[94]

In a 1982 decision, *New York v. Ferber,* the Court upheld a New York statute prohibiting the knowing promotion of sexual performances by young people under the age of sixteen.[95] Again, the Court emphasized a compelling state interest in the well-being of children.[96] A unanimous Court ruled that preventing sexual exploitation and abuse of children constitutes a government objective of surpassing importance. The justices denied First Amendment protection for child pornography, and they granted state officials greater leeway in forging statutes banning it than they enjoy regarding conventional obscenity standards.

The Court gave several reasons for distinguishing child pornography from obscenity. First, it declared a "compelling interest" in safeguarding the psychological and physical well-being of a minor.[97] The Court also saw the distribution of films and photographs depicting sexual activity by minors to be intrinsically related to the sexual abuse of children.[98] Third, the Court explained why the *Miller* standard for obscenity was not satisfactory for addressing child pornography:

> The Miller standard, like all general definitions of what may be banned as obscene, does not reflect the State's particular and more compelling interest in prosecuting those who promote the sexual exploitation of children. Thus, the question under the Miller test of whether a work, taken as a whole, appeals to the prurient interest of the average person bears no connection to the issue of whether a child has been physically or psychologically harmed in the production of the work. Similarly, a sexually explicit depiction need not be "patently offensive" in order to have required the sexual exploitation of a child for its production. In addition, a work which, taken on the whole, contains serious literary, artistic, political, scientific value may nevertheless embody the hardest core of child pornography. . . . We therefore cannot conclude that the Miller standard is a satisfactory solution to the child pornography problem.[99]

In distinguishing between child pornography and obscenity, the Court made it clear that the ruling pertains only to visual depictions and not to a particular theme or portrayal of sexual activity.[100] In sum, the Court adjusted the *Miller* formulation in the following respects: the material need not appeal to the prurient interest of the average person; the portrayal of sexual conduct need not be patently offensive; and the material at issue need not be considered as a whole.[101]

A Utah statute requiring parental notification for minors (females under the age of eighteen) seeking an abortion was upheld by the Court in 1981.[102] Here, the Court recognized legitimate state objectives of encouraging parent-child communication regarding an important medical decision. While the justices had previously struck down a parental consent law, in this case they distinguished between parental consent and parental notification.[103] This ruling suggests that minors are not necessarily mature enough to make such a decision on their own. The Court found no logical relationship between the capacity for becoming pregnant and the capacity for making a mature judgment about an abortion.[104] In 1990, the Court again upheld statutes requiring parental notification, except for those minors who successfully maneuvered the judicial bypass option.[105] This option allows a minor to persuade the judge that there are compelling reasons why parental notification is unwise. Significantly, in 1992 the Court discarded the notification/consent distinction and upheld a parental consent law with the judicial bypass option.[106]

Clearly, the cases mentioned above assigned considerable weight to the states' interest in protecting children. Yet the Court has also conferred some degree of autonomy upon minors in the area of reproductive rights. In 1977, stressing a constitutional principle of individual autonomy, the Court struck down a New York statute prohibiting the distribution of nonprescriptive contraceptives to minors under the age of sixteen years.[107] Likewise, in 1979 the Court struck down a state statute requiring parental consent for minors seeking an abortion.[108] The Court reiterated that children are not immune to constitutional protection merely on account of their age.[109]

As a whole, these sexuality rulings reveal the Court's preference for protection over autonomy. The decisions regarding pornography and obscenity justify a lower constitutional threshold in order to protect children. Given their innocence, immaturity, and vulnerability, social integration requires broad protective powers.[110]

This preference for protection is perhaps most evident in the Court's decision upholding a parental consent law. The difference between parental notification and parental consent can be seen as correspondent with the distinction between protection and autonomy. Putting the wisdom of such policies aside, a notification requirement recognizes the reasonable claim that minors may benefit from the guidance and support of their parents. Nonetheless, notification also recognizes that the ultimate decision ought to rest with the minor.

Conversely, parental consent requirements give greater weight to the protective authority of parents. (To characterize parental authority as protective is, admittedly, an arguable point.) Yet, the Court's acceptance of consent provisions does not represent a complete denial of autonomy for minors. The consent requirement was upheld only because a judicial bypass was available to minors seeking an abortion. Absent parental consent, a minor may obtain an abortion by convincing a court that she is mature and capable of giving informed consent to the proposed abortion and has, in fact, given such consent.[111] In other words, the judicial bypass affords minors the opportunity to demonstrate their capacity for autonomy. Finally, we should note that the Court presumes minors to have the autonomy to decide not to have an abortion.

Due Process

The Supreme Court's rulings pertaining to due process for minors also confer both protection and autonomy. A landmark decision regarding juvenile justice, *In re Gault,* was handed down in 1967.[112] Declaring that the Fourteenth Amendment and the Bill of Rights are not for adults alone, the Court ruled that children facing delinquency proceedings are entitled to right to counsel, notice of charges, confrontation of witnesses, and the privilege against self-incrimination.[113] Rejecting the traditional view that the juvenile's right is to custody rather than liberty, the Court recognized that, regardless of its paternalistic foundation, the juvenile justice system often produced unfair factual determinations, and inappropriate treatment.[114]

The ruling also challenged a number of other assumptions held by traditional juvenile courts and Progressive theorists concerning intervention on behalf of youth.[115] It questioned whether experts adequately pursued the best interests of children. Similarly, the Court challenged the presumption that official discretion would be guided by enlightened goals. Finally, the Court found industrial schools and reformatories resembled prisons more than educational institutions.[116]

A 1970 ruling, *In re Winship,* also extended due process protection for children.[117] Here, the Court required proof beyond a reasonable doubt for juvenile criminal cases in which minors may be deprived of their liberty.[118] The Court held that fact-finding for juvenile proceedings required the same caution expected in matters involving adults.[119] Similar to *Gault,* the Court rejected the notion that juvenile proceedings were civil actions, rather than criminal prosecutions. Here, good intentions and civil labels did not override the need for criminal due process safeguards in juvenile courts.[120]

Subsequent decisions signaled a narrowing of due process rights for children. In a 1979 ruling, *Parham v. J.R.,* the Court upheld a Georgia statute allowing the commitment of a child to a mental institution at the request of her or his parent or guardian, without a formal hearing.[121] The Court recognized the need for granting parents substantial authority over medical decisions, including institutional commitment. In a 1984 ruling, *Schall v. Martin,* the Court upheld preventive pretrial detention of juveniles, in part on the theory that they, unlike adults, are always in some form of custody.[122]

Like the sexuality cases, these due process rulings reflect a mix of protection and autonomy resulting in a lower constitutional threshold. *Gault* and *Winship* provide constitutional protection consistent with autonomy, for they challenge the presumption that adult proxies pursue the best interests of the child. Therefore, these two rulings provide children some shield from state authority, thereby making the rights of adults and minors more similar. On the other hand, the subsequent rulings recognize a substantial proxy role for adults in making critical decisions on behalf of children.[123] Accordingly, parental authority, professional expertise, and important state interests all reinforce the notion that children enjoy more protection than autonomy.

As is often the case with constitutional doctrine, we do not find a comprehensive, consistent theory or pattern in the Court's decisions, although there seems to be more weight assigned to protection than to autonomy. Many of the decisions are narrow in scope and application, for the Court has consistently refused to examine comprehensively the relationship of the minor and the state.[124] This refusal perhaps stems from the magnitude of such a task, as well as from the Court's reluctance to stray too far from the particular issues and concerns raised in a specific case. Yet, even without a comprehensive doctrine regarding the legal (or civil) status of children, Gary Melton offers the following assessment:

> The general picture of the child that emerges from recent U.S. Supreme Court opinions is of a creature who is vulnerable and incompetent and, therefore, properly subservient to the authority of parents and state. At least since 1979, decisions in children's cases have been typified by a passing (begrudging) acknowledgement that minors are "persons" entitled to the protection of the Bill of Rights, and then by extended discussions of why these rights should not be fulfilled. . . . To reach this conclusion, the Court has often had to adopt a curiously narrow vision of minors as vulnerable to all sorts of threats — except threats to their liberty or privacy.[125]

Melton's observations, while perhaps overstated, nonetheless point out the reluctance of the Court to confer constitutionally guaranteed autonomous rights on children. The rulings incorporate both integrative and autonomous rights, but not in identical fashion.

Conclusion

Children require both adult protection and autonomy from adult authority. Adult protection is necessary because youngsters are often too immature and vulnerable to make critical decisions. Children also need to experience autonomy if they are to develop into independent, responsible adults.

Child liberators offer a provocative but ultimately unpersuasive approach to establishing children's rights. For them, the best way for adults to assist children is to liberate them from oppressive adult authority and supervision. Liberators claim that adults, and adult institutions, victimize young people at every turn. But such a view overlooks the fact that many children do not experience a miserable childhood. In presenting them as innocents, and adults as demons, liberators distort and oversimplify a complicated, ambivalent, and paradoxical relationship. Girls and boys are often selfish, foolish, violent, and hateful; they are also often generous, wise, tender, and loving. Childhood, like adulthood, is typically a composite of tears and laughter, joys and sorrows, failures and triumphs. Many children experience and benefit from the love — however misguided or imperfect — of adults. Child liberators fail to recognize that adult authority does not necessarily victimize children.[126]

Child liberators also fail to acknowledge that liberation may exploit and victimize children. When liberation becomes synonymous with license, then pornography becomes sexual information and incest is considered merely an alternative sexual activity. In his classic work *The Rise and Fall of Childhood,* John Sommerville addresses the downside of children's liberation:

> Liberation, then, has often meant simply a new choice of authorities. At a time when children need adults against whom to measure themselves, they are being delivered over to their peers. Psychologists now frequently claim that the lack of involvement with role models is leading to the identity problems so characteristic of today's adolescent. Young people cannot convince themselves that they can make the transition to adulthood, because they have had so little contact with adults.[127]

Children's rights, constitutional or otherwise, ought to be forged in a cautious, thoughtful manner. Certainly, institutional and public policy reforms may help adults to more successfully fulfill their duties and responsibilities to children. The liberators' critique of the Progressive child reformers reminds us that the motives, intentions, and presumptions of child reformers have shaped subsequent institutional policies and programs. Humility and self-reflection, then, ought to guide child advocates and social reformers.

Because they inevitably fall short of their objectives and claims, reformers remain easy prey. Again, John Sommerville explains:

> It is always easy to deflate the reputations of those who are trying to make things better. Only those who are seeking to help are ever criticized for not succeeding or having mixed motives. The educators, social workers, and scoutmasters who sought to meet children's needs in a changing world were only aware of their humanitarian concern. Only in retrospect do we see that the institutionalization of childhood made growing up more difficult. With hindsight it is obvious that the rise of experts on children would lead to excessive regulation, and that there would eventually be a noisy revolt against it. But it would be a shame if we did not also recognize the goodwill of the specialists and bureaucrats who tried to ensure more humane treatment of children and the benefits which their reforms produced for many.[128]

Despite resistance by defenders of the status quo and ridicule by radicals, child reformers get on with the difficult, often thankless task of building coalitions, shaping public policy, and battling the powers that be.

Through halting, modest rulings, the Supreme Court has granted modified constitutional rights to children. Accordingly, the debate over such rights typically involves those interested in either maintaining the status quo or promoting incremental change. As is frequently the case with radical critics and visionaries, child liberators rarely see the Constitution as a means for liberating children.[129] Hence, my argument does not respond to radical critiques in any extensive manner, because we share little ground regarding the importance of First Amendment doctrine.

An intermediate constitutional status for children imperfectly entails both protection and autonomy. It embraces protective integrative rights by granting discretionary authority to the state and by recognizing important parental interests. This intermediate status also corresponds with certain autonomous rights by limiting state authority over children. However, declaring that the First Amendment ought to advance both protection and autonomy for children is merely a first step. It is like saying that children need a healthy diet. They do, but we still must determine what a healthy diet consists of, and how we may provide it.

Three

Free Speech and Public Education

Schools should strengthen our democracy by inculcating the values identified by the majority while also strengthening our

commitment to freedom by fostering

pluralism and eschewing orthodoxy in

religion or politics.

William Buss, "School Newspapers, Public Forum, and the
First Amendment"

How congruent are the aims of public education and free-speech
principles? What problems arise in reconciling the inculcative function (the transmission of values) of public schooling with free speech?
Commentators often find this relationship adversarial, so that advancing one requires hindering the other. David Diamond, for example, exalts the inculcative function and argues that, since the principal business of public education is indoctrination, our public schools
embody the denial of First Amendment rights.[1] Conversely, another
commentator concludes that the severe conflict between free speech
and inculcation requires school officials to abandon the latter.[2] Even
those who try to reconcile free speech with the inculcative function
view them as being inherently adversarial.[3] However, while tension
does exist between the aims of the First Amendment and the inculcation of values by public school officials, the relationship is more
subtle and less oppositional than is typically noted.

My examination of this relationship entails four related claims.
First, the liberal principles that underpin adult free speech are tenuous and are not presumptively valid for children. Moreover, the
aims of free speech and public education are both congruent and
conflictive. Third, the inculcative function should play an instru-
mental role in establishing student free speech. And finally, the inculcative function may serve free-speech aims. Together, these claims
lay the groundwork for a more subtle, sophisticated approach to
conferring First Amendment rights upon public school students.

Marketplace of Ideas

In general, at least five arguments defend free speech as a fundamental component of a liberal, democratic society.[4] Throughout this century, the marketplace-of-ideas argument has dominated both legal scholarship and constitutional doctrine pertaining to First Amendment free speech.[5] Some marketplace proponents argue that truth and knowledge thrive only where competing ideas collide vigorously.[6] Marketplace advocates are typically skeptical about the human capacity for distinguishing truth from falsity. For them, human fallibility implies that intellectual pluralism ought to rule the day. Justice Oliver Wendell Holmes eloquently expressed this view in a classic dissent:

> But when men have realized that time has upset many fighting faiths, they may come to believe even more than they believe the very foundations of their own conduct that the ultimate good desired is better reached by free trade in ideas — that the best test of truth is the power of the thought to get itself accepted in the competition of the market, and that truth is the only ground upon which their wishes safely can be carried out. That at any rate is the theory in our Constitution.[7]

While he is more skeptical of human rationality than is John Stuart Mill, Holmes nonetheless presumes individuals are capable of rational conduct, at least to the extent that they recognize the wisdom of the marketplace of ideas.

Marketplace proponents frequently presume that conflict, competition, and diversity are essential to liberty and are signs of societal health. The metaphor itself has special significance; just as a free-market economy is hailed by supporters for promoting social and economic goods through the pursuit of economic self-interest, so too is this intellectual marketplace expected to advance certain social goods. This free-speech argument, then, remains deeply rooted in liberal theory, and its spirit can be traced to Mill's noble defense of liberal tolerance:

> [The] peculiar evil of silencing the expression of an opinion is, that it is robbing the human race; posterity as well as the existing generation; those who dissent from the opinion, still more than those who hold it. If the opinion is right, they are deprived of the opportunity of exchanging error for truth; if wrong, they lose, what is almost as great a benefit, the clearer perception and livelier impression of truth, produced by its collision with error.[8]

Democracy

Other prominent First Amendment theorists view free speech as an essential element of democratic governance, providing citizens with the necessary information to exercise their civic duties. By prohibiting the state from restricting individual expression, free speech reinforces the notion that political authority ultimately rests with the people. Drawing heavily from the New England town meeting model of democracy, Alexander Meiklejohn, a noted proponent of this position, argues that special protection ought to be accorded political speech.[9] For him, free speech is a prerequisite for community:

> The First Amendment is not, primarily, a device for the winning of new truth, though that is very important. It is a device for the sharing of whatever truth has been won. Its purpose is to give to every voting member of the body politic the fullest possible participation in the understanding of those problems with which the citizens of a self-governing society must deal. When a free man is voting, it is not enough that the truth is known by someone else, by some scholar or administrator or legislator. The voters must have it, all of them.[10]

Self-fulfillment

While the marketplace and democratic arguments emphasize the social utility of free speech, other commentators stress the individual benefits to be gained.[11] Here, free speech plays a vital role in advancing personal development. This emphasis should hardly be surprising, since liberal theory posits human beings to be naturally striving toward moral and intellectual development. These epistemic (or self-realization) theorists declare that free speech makes a vital contribution to personal autonomy, individual self-expression, and diversity of lifestyle. Thus, state suppression of individual expression constitutes a denial of respect and dignity that is rightfully due citizens of a democratic polity. These theorists are, in large measure, more concerned with the interests of the recipients of speech than with those of the speakers.[12] Finally, such arguments often convey both intellectual relativism and moral skepticism.[13] According to Mark Yudof, these two principles are the foundations for democratic pluralism.[14]

Disutility

A fourth argument emphasizes the counterproductivity of suppressing open debate. Here, free speech is valued not merely on its own merits but because the evils of suppression ought to be avoided. Typically, three such evils are noted.[15] First, suppression of speech leads to intellectual atrophy, which is seen as a worse ill than erroneous thinking. Intellectual development is viewed as a gymnasium in which truth becomes strengthened by being compelled to defend itself against attacks, no matter how false they might be. Hence, complacent defenders of truth ought to be put on alert, for, as Mill stated, both learners and teachers go to sleep at their post as soon as there is no enemy in the field.[16]

Furthermore, disutility proponents argue that suppression of speech is counterproductive because it legitimizes false doctrine in a way that tolerance would not. Paradoxically, suppressing speech enhances its interest and appeal. As William Haley explains:

> Mankind is so constituted, moreover, that if, where expression and discussion are concerned, the enemies of liberty are met with a denial of liberty, many men of goodwill will come to suspect there is something in the proscribed doctrine after all. Erroneous doctrines thrive on being expunged. They die if exposed.[17]

Finally, these proponents claim that suppression of speech promotes social upheaval and violence. They hold that free speech furthers political participation and public dialogue. Restricting the speech of disaffected groups makes hostile actions more likely. Hence, free speech acts as a social safety valve, and its suppression exacerbates social conflict.[18]

Incompetence

The preceding arguments may be viewed as positive theories, for they share the presumption that speech has intrinsic, discernible value that merits special protection from state authority. Frederick Schauer, however, proposes an alternative theory.[19] In his view, what is uniquely special about speech is that it poses particular problems for governmental restriction. He finds government incapable of properly weighing the costs and benefits of speech suppression. Hence, there should be great distrust of government's capacity to determine truth and falsity.[20] Schauer argues, accordingly, that government restrictions tend to oversuppress speech, either out of self-interest or the inevitable slippery-slope nature of such efforts. Government incompetence, then, provides justification for protecting freedom of expression.

Liberal Speech Reconsidered

According to Glenn Tinder, classical liberal theorists, such as John Stuart Mill, rested their defense of freedom of expression upon three related principles: individualism, rationalism, and historical optimism.[21] However, sufficient scrutiny of each principle reveals a fragile and tenuous foundation for free speech. By appreciating the limitations and shortcomings of adult free-speech arguments we are better equipped to consider a defense of free speech for children.

This assessment of three fundamental liberal principles draws generously from Tinder's insightful critique of liberal tolerance. He argues that we may test these liberal principles by consulting experience through introspection. As Thomas Hobbes reminds us, each person should "read in himself, not this or that particular man; but mankind."[22] We may also consult experience by taking a historical approach in which we look outward and discern human nature in past events.[23] Accordingly, I will assess each principle by consulting experience through these two vantage points.

Individualism

Liberal theory emphasizes uniqueness and separateness with regard to human relations, and tolerance for freedom of expression has long been a component of liberalism. Tolerance of free speech, for example, was prominent in Mill's essay on liberty, which posits two spheres of human conduct, self-regarding and other-regarding.[24]

Liberal individualism pays too little attention to the fact that humans display a need for similarity by demonstrating a strong, universal impulse to join others.[25] Tinder finds this similarity impulse both inevitable and willed. It is inevitable, in large part, because the mental framework by which we interpret reality is socially constructed. For example, the very act of thinking requires an individual to share a language with others. Similarity is also willed, for we seek community, which depends upon numerous similarities. Community requires a modicum of shared values and agreement regarding social, political, and economic arrangements. Furthermore, we value similarity because it provides a basis for tradition and a link with the past. In Tinder's view,

> one cannot join with others unless he becomes like them in some respects. While community does not require the obliteration of all differences, it does depend on numerous similarities — on common experiences, common interests, and so forth. Thus, if it is man's nature to seek community, it is his nature also to seek similarity.[26]

A related criticism of liberal individualism concerns the separation of the individual from society. Such separation plays a prominent role in Mill's theory of self-regarding and other-regarding behavior. Tinder argues that for this theory to be convincing the sphere of self-regarding conduct must be so small and insignificant that it cannot make up a sphere of liberty worth caring about.[27] Furthermore, by focusing on our separateness rather than our communal character, such a view implies that concern for others is typically selfish and intrusive. Tinder finds that this perspective, when pushed too far, becomes both inhumane and misguided, for it tells us that we should be indifferent to others except where they threaten our interests.[28]

Introspection reveals us to be constantly seeking similarity, for we experience both the haunting pain of alienation and the comfort of love and friendship. A look to history reveals a universal impulse to form communities, be they tribal, civic, or religious. This striving for similarity helps explain the propensity of contemporary Americans to join others in a variety of ways, ranging from private country clubs, to twelve-step programs for recovering addicts, to activist groups fighting drunk drivers.

Rationalism

Tinder offers a twofold criticism of liberal rationalism: it overstates the degree to which human beings are rational, and it exaggerates how accessible reality is to reason. Thus, liberal free-speech proponents mistakenly conclude that truth will emerge triumphant, and an informed citizenry will take rational actions based upon sound reasoning.

How rational are human beings? While a precise answer remains beyond our grasp, by consulting experience we find ourselves to be less rational than liberalism presupposes. If we follow Hobbes's advice to "read thyself," we frequently find ourselves disturbed when our opinions are challenged, and comforted when they are accepted, by others. By and large, we do not necessarily think or act rationally when engaged in arguments over important beliefs.[29]

We also discover severe limits to human rationality when we consult history. We witness such eras as the Dark Ages and the Renaissance, the wars of religion and the Enlightenment. If humans were primarily rational beings, this ebb and flow of reason would hardly make sense. Nor do we need such a backward-looking perspective, for by examining contemporary U.S. society we also witness the disjuncture between human conduct and rational thought. Tinder notes, for example, that

> [t]here is an immense disparity between the formalities and the actualities of freedom in the United States; the range of what can legally be said is almost limitless, whereas the range of what is likely to be seriously listened to is narrow. This disparity would be inexplicable were men as rational as liberals like Locke and Mill have assumed.[30]

Tinder's challenge to liberal rationality corresponds with contemporary schools of thought. For psychoanalysis, beliefs are primarily the products of inner conflict; Marxist theory declares the primary determinant of belief to be one's economic situation; and existential-ists consider the origins of belief to lie in an irrational act of choice — a "leap" of faith. Frederick Schauer underscores the point by argu-ing that the optimistic view of human rationality embodied in the Enlightenment has been largely discredited by history and by the contemporary insights of psychology.[31]

Finally, this critique of rationalism addresses liberalism's misrep-resentation of the character of reality. Liberal theory presumes that reality is readily accessible to reason. While such a notion can ob-viously be challenged on religious grounds,[32] other contemporary schools of thought (such as phenomenology and existentialism) also question it. Disclosures of immediate experience and the conclu-sions of reason are, perhaps, radically different. As Tinder explains:

> Reason strives to bring all reality within closed systems, while experience is endless and cannot be wholly comprised in a set of rational formulas. Reason objectifies reality, but even the experience of reasoning itself includes a reality, the one who reasons — the subject — that cannot be viewed as an object, as a desk or a book can be. Reason summarizes the past, whereas immediate experience contains awareness of an undecided future.[33]

To argue that reality is not fully amenable to reason, therefore, un-dermines the liberal presumption that reason leads directly to under-standing reality.[34]

Historical Optimism

Tinder's third criticism regarding liberal free speech concerns histor-ical optimism, which implies that we not only think rationally but act rationally. This assertion applies to both individuals (as noted in the discussion regarding rationalism) and groups. For example, some argue that, when allowed to participate in a vigorous, robust debate, disgruntled groups and zealous rebels will "cool off" and not respond in an irrational, violent manner.

Through introspection, we realize that rather than living rationally we often find ourselves persistently selfish, prideful, and cunning. This may especially be the case when we are acting as part of some collective entity. Each of us can recall actions we have taken due to peer pressure, and the motives for such actions do not disappear when we move from adolescence to adulthood. Accordingly, while pursuing that which we should properly scorn, be it material goods or unrequited love, we often ignore those values and persons most dear to us. In short, in both individual and collective behavior, we are not as constructive and cooperative as liberal theory implies.

Nor do we find support for such optimism by consulting history. Instead, we find a record of war, sickness, failure, and civil turmoil. In sum, the story of the human race remains bittersweet. Whenever progress occurs, it is always tempered, and it inevitably creates an emerging set of problems. We witness, then, what Hegel referred to as a universal taint of corruption.[35] As Tinder reminds us, since we are not spontaneously orderly or spontaneously progressive, the results of our liberation are uncertain.[36] Thus, liberalism's historical optimism remains questionable.

Bringing a healthy dose of skepticism to the consideration of liberal free-speech principles has important implications for student free speech. The criticisms noted above should give us pause in considering the grounds for extending First Amendment speech protection to children. Opponents of granting free speech to public school students often stress the differences between adults and children. They argue that young people are substantially less mature, less rational, and less autonomous than their elders. Accordingly, since free speech presumes a sufficient capacity for all three facilities, it would be inappropriate to confer free speech upon children. Conversely, proponents of extending free speech to students typically emphasize the similarities between adults and children. Thus, the individual and social rewards of adult free speech are similarly assigned to children's free speech.

If Tinder's critique of liberal theory is persuasive, the arguments of both defenders and opponents of extending First Amendment protection to students need to be reconsidered. If adults are not as rational, autonomous, and individualistic as free-speech proponents claim, then to withhold free speech for students on such grounds becomes less convincing. In other words, if the liberal character of adults is overstated, then the differences between children and grown-ups are not as striking as some suggest. Likewise, if proponents of student free speech are overly optimistic about the virtues and benefits of adult free speech, then the fruits of such expression for children are similarly suspect. The limitations of liberal free-speech principles, therefore, illuminate the need for a thoughtful approach to extending free speech for children, since the similarities and differences between adults and youngsters are not the decisive factors in forging First Amendment protection for public school students.

Public Schooling: Aims and Goals

In a landmark 1954 decision regarding school segregation, the United States Supreme Court asserted that public education is perhaps the most important function of state and local government.[37] The various goals and aims assigned to public schools underscore the importance of public education. While no consensus exists in identifying educational goals, John Goodlad's classic study of public schools, *A Place Called School,* offers a convincing and comprehensive list.[38] Goodlad presents four broad areas of goals — academic, vocational, social, and personal.[39]

Academic goals entail intellectual development and mastering basic skills. Vocational goals include developing salable skills and specialized knowledge that will lead to economic independence. Social, civic, and cultural goals encompass communicating effectively in groups, obtaining knowledge about the basic workings of government, developing an awareness of one's cultural heritage, and coming to understand the necessity for moral conduct. Personal goals extend to the emotional and physical well-being of students, their creativity and aesthetic expression, and self-realization.

Free Speech and Public Education

The primary goals of public education and the aims of free speech are congruent as well as conflictive. Both free speech and public education are instruments to advance knowledge, curtail intellectual atrophy, promote an informed citizenry, further both social stability and social change, and encourage individual development.

We also witness significant conflict in the claims and assumptions underlying free speech and public education, however. For example, free speech presumes a high degree of rationality, while public education presumes a child's rational capacity requires considerable development. While free speech presumes an independent citizenry, public schooling typically minimizes student autonomy. Finally, free speech reflects substantial distrust of government authority, but public education rests upon a broad grant of state power to control and direct the intellectual and moral development of the nation's youth.

Together, such congruence and conflict suggest that establishing free speech for public school students faces significant, but not insurmountable, obstacles. In forging First Amendment protection for students, we should remember that children need a mix of protection and autonomy. Therefore, special attention must be given to the inculcative function of public schooling, a significant source of tension in student speech disputes.

Inculcation of Values

Defenders and opponents of the inculcative function typically describe it in either benign or catastrophic terms. Defenders imply that the inculcative function merely refers to the transmission of values, which is inherent in the educational enterprise.[40] Critics characterize it as indoctrination unbefitting public education in a liberal democracy.[41] Neither view, however, offers much help for examining the First Amendment rights of public school students. The benign approach minimizes the tension between inculcation and free speech, while the indoctrination claim overstates the conflict. The inculcative function entails something more than the mere transmission of values, and something less than a totalitarian pedagogical weapon. It includes the transmission of preferred values aimed at the social integration of students. In addition, inculcation employs a system of rewards, penalties, and modeling by school officials. Finally, it involves both curriculum and student conduct.

The inculcative function remains an intrinsic part of public schooling because pedagogy entails moral and ethical decisions. By discouraging students from cheating on exams or stealing personal belongings from lockers, school officials inculcate values. By making grades dependent upon hard work, educators transmit values. In promoting an appreciation of the human struggle regarding civil rights and individual liberties, civics teachers instill values in students.

The inculcative function is also willed, for public educators explicitly pass on a set of norms to students. Such values may include fairness, honesty, respect for democracy, and disapproval of criminal violence. Others would argue that a "hidden curriculum" instills the values of obedience, passivity, inequality, and conformity.[42] In sum, the inculcative function permeates public education, as it must and as it should.[43]

Inculcation, then, serves the stated aims of public education. For example, an academic goal identified by Goodlad is the development of "positive attitudes" toward intellectual activity, including curiosity and a desire for further learning. Clearly, this aim is consistent with the inculcative function.

Inculcation also furthers the vocational aims of public education. When public schools cultivate competitiveness, self-reliance, obedience, and promptness, they are promoting values sought in the workplace. Similarly, the socialization of the future worker requires the transmission of economic values rooted in the pervasive sorting, measurement, and classification that students are subjected to. Educators encourage pupils to develop a strong work ethic, and public schooling inculcates this ethic with a system of rewards and punishments.

The civic goals of public education presume a desired set of values and principles: democracy is the preferred form of government; citizenship entails duties and responsibilities, as well as rights and privileges; and social and political stability is preferable to chaos. When the inculcative function transmits such values and principles, it serves the civic goals of public education. Similarly, these goals imply the need to train children to join a democratic citizenry. In sum, the inculcative function furthers the civic aims of public education by instilling preferred values and by training students to conduct themselves properly.

The social aims of public education may also be served by the inculcation of values. If schools are to advance social reform, there must be a shared sense of what a particular social ill is, along with agreement on what ought to be done. For example, if schools are expected to alleviate racism, than children ought to understand why racism is deplorable. Therefore, training students to conduct themselves in nonracist fashion while on school grounds furthers both the inculcative function and social goals. Public schools cannot advance a social agenda without inculcating a set of values, for both social stability and social change require a core set of shared principles. As Andrew Oldenquist explains:

> A society is a moral community, which means that it has a shared morality that predictably regulates interpersonal conduct. This morality is internalized, and operates in the absence of police or threatened social disapproval far more effectively than cynics believe. . . . To suggest that a society lacks the right to teach children the basic morality on which its very existence depends is tantamount to suggesting that it has no right to exist.[44]

Hence, shared notions of justice, fairness, dignity, and equality are essential for sustaining a democratic, pluralistic society,[45] and it is reasonable to expect our public schools to inculcate such values.[46] Of course, the scope, extent, and quality of inculcation raise important questions and concerns, for this function, if pressed too aggressively, becomes a means of thought control.

Finally, the inculcative function serves the personal goals of public education. Children typically pass through developmental stages that are primarily socially determined. Self-fulfillment, self-realization, and individual autonomy require societal markers in order to have meaning, and inculcation is invaluable in directing the developmental process so that a child becomes a particular type of adult.

The Inculcative Function and Free Speech

Because inculcation is so important in public education, it receives considerable attention from commentators and federal courts alike. For many, the function is a primary reason that the constitutional rights of students should be considerably less extensive than those of adults. However, the inculcative function is not completely at odds with free speech, and exaggerating their conflict mistakenly compels us to choose between them. Such a choice must be made at times, but in many other situations we find that although serving one there is little conflict with the other. Therefore, we should neither minimize nor exaggerate the degree of congruence or conflict between the inculcative function and the extension of constitutional free speech to students.

There are several points of tension and conflict between the First Amendment and the inculcative function. While the Constitution protects critics of the state, inculcation frequently promotes respect for it in two ways. First, students are required to obey the wishes and commands of school officials. In addition, students are typically inculcated to respect adult authorities, including parents, teachers, employers, and political leaders.[47] This inculcation may be pursued in various ways, ranging from the teaching of U.S. history to the playing of the national anthem at sporting events. Thus, by protecting dissenting voices, the First Amendment may be at odds with the respect for state authority public educators seek to inculcate.

Defenders of the First Amendment argue that social discord must frequently be the price of liberty, since the Constitution protects expression that exacerbates social cleavages. Therefore, we must tolerate Nazis marching in Skokie, Illinois (a city with a substantial Jewish population), and allow protesters to burn the flag.[48] Conversely, educators strive to minimize classroom discord by vigorously regulating student conduct.[49]

The First Amendment conveys a strong distrust of government's capacity to make normative judgments regarding speech. Distrust of government, however, seems antithetical to the inculcative function, which confers a large measure of discretionary authority upon local school officials.[50] Public educators make a broad range of normative judgments about both student conduct and school curriculum.

Similarly, in presuming human fallibility, the First Amendment encourages moral skepticism. However, the inculcative function rejects this view by advancing a set of preferred values. Thus, free speech promotes a diverse marketplace of ideas, while inculcation encourages students to share certain views and to behave in a conformed manner.

Free speech protects the flow of information, thereby ensuring an informed citizenry as well as a marketplace of ideas. The inculcative function, however, impedes the flow of information in two ways. First, school officials may restrict or prohibit student expression they deem to be disruptive, offensive, or disrespectful. Second, school officials restrict student access to information. For example, educators exclude or remove books from the school library, restrict the content of classroom materials, or prohibit certain groups and speakers from addressing students. Some commentators also argue that the First Amendment includes a "right to belief" that forbids government indoctrination. However, because it entails a strong dose of indoctrination, the inculcative function invariably collides with the claim that this right applies to students.

However, despite considerable conflict and tension, there is also significant congruence between the inculcative function and free speech, or at least considerable opportunity for them to be allies as well as adversaries. For example, free speech advances a host of liberal values that school officials may also inculcate. The values to be inculcated are not set in concrete, so that when schools promote appreciation of liberty, autonomy, rationality, popular sovereignty, and human fallibility they also serve free speech.

In addition, political dialogue requires at least a modicum of civility from both speaker and audience. Hence, the First Amendment leaves libel, defamation, and "fighting words" unprotected. The inculcative function, by promoting civility and respect for others, helps students understand the assaultive character of certain types of expression. Therefore, by inculcating civility educators serve both free speech and the inculcative function.

A final point of congruence regards the manner in which educators inculcate values. Certainly, the First Amendment restricts state censorship. While coercive censorship may play an important, even prominent role in the inculcative function, other avenues more amenable to free speech remain available. For example, educators may inculcate values through rigorous inquiry. By critically discussing issues like racism, the virtues of equality may be inculcated without authoritarian censorship. Similarly, by practicing and demonstrating the values to be inculcated, such as tolerance, educators set an example for students to follow. In sum, public educators may inculcate in noncoercive ways, thereby reducing the tension between free speech and the inculcative function.

Conclusion

> [So] long as the First Amendment is thought to be derived
> from principles of liberalism and the belief in the self-sufficient
> and autonomous individual, value training and community
> concerns will conflict with free speech.[51]

The stage has been set for a detailed analysis of the First Amendment rights of public school students. We have identified the main defenses of liberal free speech and have reconsidered core liberal principles to temper the claims of both proponents and opponents of granting students First Amendment protection. In addition, we have acknowledged the tension between the aims of public education and free speech. Finally, we have placed the inculcative function at center stage, since it has been a focal point in the debate.

The importance of the inculcative function illuminates a central paradox regarding education founded on liberal principles. Liberalism is, at its core, decidedly antipaternalistic; on the other hand, public education, at least in practice, is highly paternalistic. The former presumes a high degree of autonomy and rationality, while the latter presumes the opposite. This paradox suggests that the inculcative function, however important, should not serve as justification for wholesale denial of First Amendment rights to students. As Walter Kamiat observes:

> The need to induct children into the community justifies both limiting the application of the first amendment to children and allowing a highly active state role in education. But the education process must ensure that the adults it produces see themselves as capable of relatively autonomous choice because this self-perception is essential to their effective performance of their social roles. This latter consideration justifies limiting the state's indoctrinative powers and recognizing some degree of first amendment protection for children.[52]

Given this paradox, reconciling the inculcative function with the First Amendment remains a formidable task. The chapters that follow suggest how such a reconciliation can be achieved.

Four

A Focused Balancing Alternative

Our objection to public forum analysis is not

that it invariably yields wrong results

(although it sometimes does), but that it

distracts attention from the first

amendment values at stake in a given

case. . . . Classifying a medium of

communication as a public forum may

cause legitimate governmental interests

to be thoughtlessly brushed aside;

classifying it as something other than

a public forum may lead courts to ignore

the incompatibility of the challenged

regulations with first amendment

values.

Daniel Farber and John Nowak, "The Misleading Nature of
Public Forum Analysis"

Building a principled foundation for extending First Amendment
protection to public school students requires an examination of the
types of First Amendment problems confronting the federal courts
and the prevailing doctrines employed by the bench to resolve them.
This foundation also requires replacing public forum analysis with a
"focused balancing" alternative. Finally, we need to clarify what we
mean by "student speech."

**Problem One: Content Regulation and
Definitional Balancing**

There are three basic types of First Amendment problems. One concerns the complete prohibition of a message or a category of speech, where the state restricts ideas or information. For example, government officials may censor publications critical of the state, or state legislators might forbid the teaching of a foreign language in public schools.[1] Although the core command of the First Amendment is a prohibition on censorship, the courts have never considered this command to be absolute, either in theory or in practice.[2] The prevailing approach taken in reviewing direct state censorship entails "definitional balancing."[3] It recognizes that not all speech merits constitutional protection, for the right to certain utterances may be outweighed by legitimate state interests. This definitional approach identifies categories of speech — obscenity, defamation, child pornography, and false or misleading commercial speech — that do not warrant First Amendment protection.[4]

Definitional balancing entails three related inquiries. The first examines to what extent the state infringes upon constitutionally protected speech. If no such infringement occurs, than the court applies a rationality test that typically permits the restriction to stand. If, however, the state infringes unduly on protected speech, then a second inquiry is triggered. Here, the state must show that the restriction serves a compelling state interest that outweighs the First Amendment values threatened by the regulation. A strict standard of review is employed, which invalidates the most direct and blatant state censorship efforts. If, however, the state convinces the court that the restriction serves a compelling interest, a third judicial inquiry is made. Here, the court determines whether the state regulation is "narrowly tailored," so that means and ends are sufficiently linked. Together, these inquiries constitute a strict standard of review that makes content-based regulations of protected speech presumptively invalid.[5]

Problem Two: Time, Place, and Manner Regulations

A second basic First Amendment problem concerns state efforts to impose content-neutral regulations on the time, place, or manner of constitutionally protected speech. Here, the state incidentally restricts the flow of ideas and information while pursuing other goals. For example, governments may prohibit the use of loudspeakers in residential areas or impose ceilings on campaign contributions.[6] Because they are content neutral, such regulations are seen to pose a lesser threat to First Amendment values than do content-based measures, for they do not necessarily discriminate against a particular viewpoint. Nonetheless, because such restrictions infringe upon protected speech, judicial scrutiny is required.

The prevailing judicial attitude toward content-neutral regulations is the "time, place, and manner doctrine." It detects content-based restrictions, and switches them to the rigorous analysis employed in definitional balancing. Moreover, the doctrine prevents content-neutral regulations from substantially limiting opportunities to receive or transmit information effectively.[7]

To fulfill these functions, the doctrine employs a three-prong test. First, the regulation must be deemed content neutral, both in language and operation. In addition, the regulation must be narrowly tailored to serve a significant government interest. Finally, the regulation must leave open ample alternative channels of communication. This doctrine, then, entails balancing the extent to which communicative activity is in fact inhibited against the rights, values, or interests served by the regulation.[8]

This balancing has two important variables. One involves the degree to which the restriction falls unevenly on various groups in the society. For example, a regulation that restricts the distribution of handbills would disproportionately affect groups with sparse financial resources. A second variable concerns the degree to which the restriction shuts down places traditionally considered, or formally designated, to be public forums.[9] While this level of review

may be somewhat less rigorous than definitional balancing, it nonetheless requires the regulation to be content neutral, narrowly tailored, and pursuant of a significant public interest.[10]

Problem Three: Situational Regulations

A third censorship problem involving the First Amendment springs
from situational regulations in which the state action, although content based, applies only to particular locations or specific speakers.
No complete suppression of speech occurs, since only certain speech
situated in a particular social or physical environment is restricted.[11]
Such restraints focus upon a defined category of speech and its
harmful effects on a specific environment. An example of a situational regulation would be a school board prohibiting public school
students (while on school grounds) from wearing armbands to protest the Vietnam War.

Situational regulations receive a distinct standard of review. They
pose less threat to First Amendment values than does complete censorship, since most individuals are unaffected and most physical
environments remain open. However, these restrictions may result
in the government either negligently or deliberately censoring a particular viewpoint. Therefore, a demanding standard of review is
needed to ensure that situational restraints do not become the func-
tional equivalent of censorship.[12]

For situational restraints, public forum analysis remains the prevailing approach taken by the courts. Unlike definitional balancing,
content-based restrictions are not presumptively invalid. The validity of content-based restrictions depends primarily upon the location (or forum) of the restricted speech.

Public forum analysis delineates three types of speech forums.[13]
"By long tradition or by government fiat," certain locations (e.g.,
public parks or sidewalks) are considered classic or quintessential
speech forums.[14] Regulation of protected speech occurring at such
sites receives strict scrutiny as a result of the special character of the

location. If the state action is content based, the courts use definitional balancing; if it is content neutral, then the time, place, and
manner doctrine is employed. Either way, restrictions on speech in
classic public forums are rarely upheld by the courts.

A second type of forum is public property that the state has
opened for use as a place for expressive activity (e.g., a convention
center owned or controlled by a city).[15] The same doctrines employed for classic public forums are operative for such designated
public forums. Although the state is not required to retain the open
character of the facility, so long as it does it is bound by the same
standards that apply to a traditional public forum.[16]

A third category consists of nonpublic forums. Typically, these
are properties owned or controlled by the government, such as mili-
tary installations. Here, speech restrictions receive less stringent judicial scrutiny, for the courts apply a rationality test that presumptively permits the state regulations to stand.[17]

Public Forum Doctrine Reconsidered

Public school regulations restricting student expression are typically
hybrid or situational in character, since they are often content based.
For example, school officials have restricted particular ideas and
viewpoints, such as opposition to the Vietnam War.[18] Furthermore,
school regulations are specifically directed at students, and they typically apply only to student speech occurring on school grounds.[19]

Daniel Farber and John Nowak correctly note two key problems
with public forum analysis.[20] First, by classifying a medium of communication as a public forum, the courts may ignore legitimate government interests. Conversely, when courts declare a medium of
communication to be something other than a public forum, they
may devalue the First Amendment.[21] Hence, public forum analysis
directs our attention to places at the expense of significant government interests and First Amendment values.[22]

Public forum analysis is especially ill-suited for public school regulations. Due to the inculcative function, the special status of children, and the aims of public education, disputes involving student speech warrant an intermediate level of judicial scrutiny. Yet, when the courts find public schools to be designated public forums, content-based restrictions become presumptively invalid, and a rigorous standard of review is employed. Such exacting judicial scrutiny may mistakenly undervalue legitimate state interests, including the inculcative function. Conversely, when the courts declare public schools to be nonpublic forums, they apply a rationality test that may insufficiently weigh the First Amendment.

Public forum analysis, then, lacks precision for accommodating the array of disputes concerning student speech. Taking this approach produces confused and tortured opinions in which the courts struggle to discern the appropriate forum category for stadiums, auditoriums, school-sponsored newspapers, and faculty mail systems.[23] Clearly, an alternative to public forum analysis is needed.[24]

Focused Balancing

In place of public forum analysis, Farber and Nowak offer a provocative "focused balancing" approach, which entails three related requirements.[25] First, an articulation requirement stresses the clarity and specificity of regulations. The government must set out clearly what speech is permissible (or the converse), the goals the regulation seeks to achieve, and how these goals are related to the context and the affected category of speech. The government's aim should not be an after-the-fact rationalization, and this requirement is supposed to ensure that censorship is not the primary purpose of the regulation.[26]

Second, a permissibility requirement demands that the government show how the regulatory goal is related to the specific location and to the kind of speech being regulated.[27] This requirement serves as a check on improper motivation and ensures a focused legislative judgment.[28] Accordingly, the goals must be consistent with First

Amendment values, which usually means no viewpoint discrimination is permitted.

Finally, a balancing requirement compels the state to demonstrate how the regulation serves a governmental interest that outweighs its impact on speech.[29] Here, the courts are to examine the relationship between the goal and the regulation, with two important caveats. First, the court must weigh the "entire class of speech," not merely the interest of the individual party before the court. This requirement seeks to prevent ad hoc situational regulations from becoming a cover for outright censorship.[30] Second, the court must keep in mind the "profound national commitment" to free speech by employing a "thumb on the scales" approach that favors the First Amendment.[31]

Together, these three requirements guide the court in determining whether the regulated expression has an impact on its social or physical environment different from other types of expression. This approach also allows judicial review for determining if such restrictions interfere with a legitimate societal interest unrelated to censorship.[32] Admittedly, it will not resolve all cases or settle all First Amendment issues. While focused balancing may be an improvement over public forum analysis, Farber and Nowak caution that it should not be considered a panacea for the problematic character of hybrid or situational regulations.[33] Nonetheless, this approach succeeds in illuminating the difficulties in forging First Amendment protection for student speech. Thus, its merit lies not so much in the results it produces as in the questions and concerns it raises.

Constitutional Persons: *Tinker* and Students

In a landmark 1967 ruling, *In re Gault,* the United States Supreme Court announced that children possess qualified independent constitutional protection with regard to criminal justice.[34] Two years later, in *Tinker v. Des Moines,* the Court extended constitutional protection to children by granting them qualified First Amendment rights inside the schoolhouse gate. Together, *Tinker* and *Gault* declared that the constitutional rights of children would no longer be solely dependent upon adult proxies.

The impact of *Tinker* on education law in general, and students' rights in particular, has been dramatic. In Thomas Flygare's view,

> [Tinker] ushered in the student rights movement of the 1970s and had a powerful impact on subsequent court decisions in hundreds of cases touching on political expression. Tinker was like a great athlete appearing in an obscure sport — like a Mary Lou Retton or a Greg Louganis — because it brought instant visibility and respectability to a previously isolated endeavor. Tinker simply demanded that the nation begin to pay some attention to school law.[35]

Given the historic and doctrinal importance of *Tinker,* a descriptive summation of the case is helpful.

In December 1965, three students in Des Moines, Iowa (aged thirteen, fifteen, and sixteen), attended public school wearing black armbands to protest U.S. involvement in the Vietnam War. Just before their action, the city's public school principals had adopted a policy stating that students engaged in such actions would be asked to remove their armbands; if they refused, they would be suspended until they returned to school without them. The three students were suspended from school indefinitely for defying this policy.

The students subsequently brought suit against the Des Moines school district, claiming that the officials' actions violated the First Amendment guarantee of free speech. They sought an injunction restraining the suspensions and also asked for nominal damages. The district court dismissed the complaint, applying a "reasonable standard" to the actions taken by the school officials.[36] The Eighth Circuit Court of Appeals affirmed the lower court's ruling.[37]

The United States Supreme Court held, in a seven to two decision, that the actions taken by the Des Moines school officials violated the First Amendment rights of the students.[38] Writing for the majority,

Justice Abe Fortas declared that the students' actions were "akin to 'pure speech,'" which is protected by the First Amendment.[39] Accordingly, the Court held that while school officials are rightfully accorded wide latitude in maintaining discipline and order in the classroom, such authority is not unlimited.[40] Students do possess certain First Amendment rights inside the classroom, so long as they do not cause "material disruption" of classwork or "substantial infringement" of the rights of others.[41] The majority emphasized that the students' actions constituted passive, nondisruptive, political expression. Finally, the Court made clear that its ruling did not address the constitutional validity of dress codes, hair-length regulations, or other matters regarding decorum.[42]

This extension of First Amendment rights to public school students raised grave concerns for the two dissenting justices. Justice Harlan argued that the Court should have granted "good faith" deference to the school officials.[43] Justice Hugo Black offered a scathing, blistering rebuke of the majority opinion. He maintained that the Court's decision was a completely unwarranted intrusion into the workings of local public schools.[44] Furthermore, he held that the ruling transferred control of the public schools from elected officials to federal judges and students.[45] Black also claimed that the ruling was reminiscent of the infamous substantive due process decisions employed by the Court earlier in the century, and he reminded his brethren of the consequences stemming from such illegitimate interference.[46]

The *Tinker* ruling asserted three related claims that subsequently laid the foundation for constitutional free speech for students. First, the Court explicitly declared them to be "persons" under the Constitution. Students possess fundamental rights that the state must respect, and they, in turn, must respect their obligations to the state. Government must view students as constitutional persons, rather than as "closed-circuit recipients" of communication chosen by the state.[47] The Court's declaration that students are constitutional persons was both remarkable and significant. This view collided with the commonly held premise that free speech presupposes a level of maturity and autonomy that children do not enjoy.[48] Thus, *Tinker* directly challenged the prevailing logic of First Amendment doctrine.[49]

Second, the Court found school officials to be bound by the Constitution. Citing prior decisions, the Court held that the Fourteenth Amendment protects the citizen against the state and all of its creatures, including boards of education. The important, delicate, and highly discretionary functions carried out by school officials must be performed within the limits of the Bill of Rights, because schools ought to teach young people that important principles of our government are not mere platitudes.[50]

While emphasizing the importance of public education, the Court also warned public educators that they do not possess absolute authority over their students and that public schools are not to become "enclaves of totalitarianism."[51] Accordingly, public education should not foster a homogeneous people.[52] Rather, the Court reiterated a view of public schools expressed in a 1967 decision regarding academic freedom for teachers:

> The vigilant protection of constitutional freedoms is nowhere
> more vital than in the community of American schools. . . .
> The classroom is peculiarly the "marketplace of ideas." The
> Nation's future depends upon leaders trained through wide ex-
> posure to that robust exchange of ideas which discovers truth
> "out of a multitude of tongues, [rather] than through any kind
> of authoritative selection."[53]

Third, the Court declared that the primacy of classroom discipline and order established the boundaries for constitutionally protected student expression. Thus, student speech that "materially disrupts" classwork or involves "substantial disorder or invasion of the rights of others" is not protected by the First Amendment.[54] The Court stressed the passive, silent character of the armbands, concluding that they resulted in negligible disruption of school decorum.[55] Disruption, then, becomes the litmus test for student free speech. School officials must demonstrate that their forecast of disruption does not rest upon "undifferentiated fear."[56] In order to punish students "after the fact," school officials must show that the speech substantially disrupted the school.[57]

Farber and Nowak note the congruence between the *Tinker* ruling and the focused balancing test.[58] Their articulation requirement corresponds with *Tinker*'s command that school officials base their forecasts of disruption on something more than "undifferentiated fear." The permissibility requirement corresponds with *Tinker*'s prohibition of viewpoint discrimination. Finally, the balancing requirement corresponds with the significant weight *Tinker* assigns to classroom order and discipline. Thus, the focused balancing approach is exemplified in the *Tinker* decision.

Parameters of Student Speech

Tinker explicitly protected "pure speech," or direct linguistic communication.[59] Lower courts have concurred, granting broad protection for student "underground newspapers."[60] The ruling also conferred constitutional protection on symbolic speech that is closely akin to pure speech.[61] The Court, however, failed to extend protection to "speech plus" conduct, such as student dress, hairstyle, and decorum. Nor did the decision address aggressive, disruptive action or group demonstrations.[62]

Tinker understood that "speech plus" frequently disrupts the routine operation of schools by diverting the attention of students and officials. In addition, "speech plus" makes it difficult to separate student expression from disruptive, disobedient conduct. The following cases illustrate why courts are properly reluctant to extend First Amendment protection to such disputes.[63]

In the fall of 1968, to protest the playing of "Dixie" during a pep rally, a group of black high school students conducted a silent walkout. This incident occurred in a recently integrated Arkansas school system experiencing considerable racial strife. Following their suspension, the students brought suit charging, among other things, that the walkout was "speech" protected by the First Amendment. The district court held that there was no federal question involved, and the complaint was dismissed. The Eighth Circuit Court of Appeals affirmed this judgment, concluding that such conduct was not a constitutionally protected form of dissent.[64] Conceding that the action was primarily "speech," the court explicitly distinguished this type of student expression from the *Tinker* armbands. While these were rightfully considered akin to "pure speech," the court judged the pep rally walkout to constitute the aggressive, disruptive group action explicitly left unprotected in *Tinker*.[65]

In a 1972 ruling, *Gebert v. Hoffman,* a federal district court established guidelines for determining when "speech plus" crosses the disruption threshold established by *Tinker*.[66] In this case, school officials had suspended thirty-six high school students for engaging in sit-in demonstrations during and after school hours. Referring to the rejection of a "heckler's veto" established in *Terminiello v. Chicago,* the court stated that only the "conduct of the demonstrators and not the reaction of the audience" should be considered.[67] Accordingly, the court found the sit-ins to be unprotected speech because they entailed students being absent from class, thereby unduly disrupting the normal operation of the school.

The courts also confront the problematic distinction between speech and action. On occasion, judges struggle to determine whether the object of official punishment is student expression or defiant conduct. For example, in *Schwartz v. Schuker,* Jeffrey Schwartz (a high school student) distributed an independent student newspaper, *High School Free Press,* off school grounds but near school property.[68] Like many underground publications, it was highly critical of school administrators. The principal advised Schwartz that no distribution of the newspaper on school premises would be tolerated. Subsequently, a substantial number of copies were found in his possession while he was on school grounds. Although Schwartz was not accused of distributing the newspapers, he was ordered to surrender the copies he possessed to the dean. He not only refused to comply with the order but advised another student to follow his lead and dis-

obey the dean. As a result of this defiance, he was formally suspended.
Defying the suspension, Schwartz appeared on school grounds a few
days later. In upholding the actions of the school officials, the federal
district court expressed confusion regarding his suspension:

> [It] is far from clear . . . that Jeffrey was suspended because of
> protected activity under the First Amendment rather than fla-
> grant and defiant disobedience of the school authorities. While
> his action might have also included actual or threatened dis-
> semination of the paper on or off school premises, his conduct
> went much further.[69]

The court's confusion is understandable, for defiance is often a
crucial component of student expression. For example, the students
in *Tinker* defied officials by wearing their armbands to school. If the
courts are to sever defiance from student expression, as the court did
in *Schwartz,* they must make sure that such separation does not
serve as a ruse for squelching legitimate student expression.

Although a particular ruling may be unconvincing, and the
speech/conduct dichotomy is imperfect, a distinction must be made
between action that is primarily "speech" and that which is not.
Without such a distinction, either student speech would be even
more precariously protected or school officials would be unduly
restricted in their legitimate efforts to regulate the conduct of students. Accordingly, the courts have been willing to protect "pure
speech," and to some extent "symbolic speech," but they have been
most reluctant to bring "speech plus" directly under First Amendment protection. My examination of scores of federal court decisions reveals no instance in which student demonstrations, sit-ins,
and walkouts have been declared immune from state punishment.[70]

In general, "speech plus" disputes receive scant attention in this
book for two reasons. First, many student demonstrations of various sorts are intentionally disruptive. While such actions raise important issues and concerns about educational policy, they presumptively fail the disruptive standard imposed by *Tinker* and do not

present formidable difficulties for the court. Simply put, they presumptively fall beyond the reach of the First Amendment. Second, to keep this inquiry focused and manageable, "speech plus" disputes regarding dress, hairstyle, and decorum are not considered. These cases also raise important issues regarding disciplinary authority, educational policy, and, arguably, constitutional rights. However, similar to disputes involving religious speech, they warrant detailed discussion not possible here.

Conclusion

Public forum analysis remains ill-suited for resolving student speech disputes, for it either improperly ignores legitimate state interests or it fails to adequately protect free-speech principles. It lacks the necessary precision for weighing the inculcative function, the varied character of student speech, and the special role of public education. In sum, the categorical framework set forth in *Perry* fails to provide an intermediate level of judicial scrutiny.

Conversely, Farber and Nowak's focused balancing approach seems better suited for protecting student speech. Its three requirements — articulation, permissibility, and balancing — provide greater precision and sensitivity in reconciling the First Amendment and the inculcative function.

With these points in mind, let us now consider the issues surrounding the toleration of direct, linguistic communication (including symbolic speech) by public school students.

Five

Tolerating Student Speech

Tolerance is a complex psychological state. Every society, just like every individual, must develop methods of coping with behavior that manifests ways of thinking regarded as objectionable but which, for one reason or another, simply must be tolerated. Some way of thinking must be constructed that

will assist those who have to be tolerant in

dealing with the impulses and internal doubts

about their own identity that are raised by

the troublesome behavior. . . . The

techniques and responses vary greatly, but

which techniques and responses are

selected will indicate much about the group

that selects them. In this society the

terminology of "rights" sometimes seems to

perform this sort of separating oneself from

the acts of others, which is usually an

important predicate for tolerance.

Lee C. Bollinger, *The Tolerant Society*

Student free-speech disputes, in large measure, arise in three contexts. Some disputes concern the refusal by school officials to permit or tolerate certain speech. Others involve incidents in which school officials decline to associate the public schools with certain types of student speech. A third area relates to efforts by school officials to control student access to adult expression. These three categories of disputes are distinguished by what students ask (or demand) of school officials. These categorical distinctions are important, for the character of the dispute shapes the First Amendment protection for student speech.

Toleration

Disputes between students and educators often arise when school officials refuse to tolerate student expression. Such toleration may be understood as a continuum of restraint. At one end, tolerance is merely the absence of coercion and punishment. Here, school officials need not be silent or neutral toward the student speech. Rather, they refrain from exercising their authority in a punitive or prohibitive manner. At the other end, tolerance entails a more neutral stance. Besides not punishing students, educators ignore, or at the very least feign indifference toward, the student expression.

This category of disputes entails student demands that school officials "do nothing." In other words, students wish to express themselves without fear of punishment. Such requests are hardly benign, for student speech may undermine the authority of school officials (as when underground newspapers criticize them harshly). Students, then, who ask school officials to "do nothing" may be asking a great deal.

Association

By requesting access to school resources and facilities, students seek the direct assistance of officials in furthering their expression. As just indicated, these requests are not necessarily benign. Because student speech is often controversial and occasionally repugnant, public educators must grapple with the fact that, for many, their association with such expression implies endorsement. Accordingly, association, like toleration, may be viewed as a continuum. At one end, association is synonymous with permission. It does not infer endorsement, since school officials may "associate" with student speech while disavowing the expression. For example, they might allow a controversial article in the school newspaper, but make it clear that the article does not represent the views or policies of the school administration. The other end of the association continuum involves active support, and even endorsement, of student expression. For example, officials might encourage or explicitly support a school-sponsored newspaper article aimed at combating drug use by young people. What often distinguishes these disputes from those involving toleration is the level of assistance given by school officials.

Indoctrination

A third area of disputes regards a corollary student right to receive ideas and information. This right presumes that the First Amendment entails both the right to speak and the right to hear, thereby ensuring the free flow of information and ideas. These kinds of disputes typically arise when school officials restrict student access or exposure to certain ideas or information. Unlike the other two categories, these disputes often involve adult expression, such as classroom texts, library books, and films. Thus, indoctrination disputes typically involve adult speech, rather than student speech as such.

Articulation Requirement

Focused balancing, an alternative to public forum analysis, yields significant First Amendment protection for students engaged in independent, nondisruptive speech. Its articulation requirement imposes three demands upon school officials who want to regulate student speech. First, they must clearly articulate what speech is proscribed. Second, officials must identify the regulatory goals. Finally, they have to articulate how these goals are related to public schools and the affected category of speech. Together, these three demands address the ills of overly broad and vague school regulations, which have an indirect chilling effect upon legitimate student speech that merits First Amendment protection. Similarly, vague regulations deny students of reasonable notice about the possible consequences of their speech. Thus, overly broad and vague speech regulations may trap the innocent student, as well as inviting arbitrary and discriminatory enforcement by allowing school officials to "cast too wide a net."

Satisfying the articulation requirement is no easy task, since clarity, like beauty, often lies in the eye of the beholder. Nonetheless, two general principles should guide school officials who wish to restrict student speech. First, the articulation requirement demands that speech regulations go beyond generalities. Second, with few exceptions, school restrictions may not extend beyond the school grounds. Both principles have found support in the courts.

In *Sullivan v. Houston Independent School District,* a federal court rightly declared that generalities may not serve as standards of behavior.[1] The following school rule served as the basis for expelling two high school seniors for their involvement in the production and distribution of an underground newspaper that criticized school officials: The "school principal may make such rules and regulations that may be necessary in the administration of the school and in promoting its best interests, he may enforce obedience to any reasonable and lawful command."[2] Such a rule fails to supply objective standards by which a student may assess his or her behavior or by which a school official may evaluate the behavior. The federal district court correctly found the regulation to be unconstitutional for both vagueness and overbreadth.[3] The court's ruling is congruent with the articulation requirement. The school regulation fails to meet this test on all counts, since the administrators failed to set forth clearly what speech is restricted, the specific goals of the regulation, or how these goals relate to the affected category of speech.

The generality principle also requires that school officials do more than merely paraphrase a constitutional standard articulated in a Supreme Court decision. For example, in *Jacobs v. Board of School Commissioners,* Indianapolis school officials prohibited the distribution of a student underground newspaper on school grounds, based upon this rule:

> No student shall distribute in any school any literature that
> is . . . either by its content or by the manner of distribution it-
> self, productive of, or likely to produce a significant disruption
> of the normal educational processes, functions or purposes in
> any of the Indianapolis schools, or injury to others.[4]

The school officials defended this rule because of its similarity to *Tinker.* The Seventh Circuit Court of Appeals correctly rejected this argument, declaring that paraphrasing a constitutional standard is not sufficiently specific.[5]

The generality principle has not been embraced by all federal courts, however. In *Eisner v. Stamford Board of Education,* the Second Circuit Court of Appeals declared the following school regulation to be constitutionally permissible:[6]

> No material shall be distributed which, either by its content or
> by the manner of distribution itself, will interfere with the
> proper and orderly operation and discipline of the school, will
> cause violence or disorder, or will constitute an invasion of the
> rights of others.[7]

While acknowledging that the standard of "invasion of the rights of others" is not a model of clarity or preciseness, the court argued that school rules may be more vague than would be allowed in other contexts.[8] According to the court, three mitigating factors permit this level of vagueness and generality. First, the school rule does not authorize punishment of students. Second, the rule only applies to students on school property during school hours. Finally, the rule does not close alternative channels of distribution outside school property.[9]

Similarly, in *Bystrom v. Fridley,* the Eighth Circuit Court of Appeals explained why school regulations need not be as exacting as the criminal code.[10] In upholding a rule that restricted the distribution of written material on school premises, the circuit court noted that some of the wording in the regulation was much more general than is customary in many areas of the law. Nonetheless, the court justified granting school officials greater leeway than is typically afforded elected legislators:

> [We] must remember that a high degree of generality is made necessary by the subject matter. The concepts involved (indecency, vulgarity, likelihood of material disruption) are general by their very nature. But violation of these guidelines does not subject anyone to criminal sanctions, nor do they apply to the public at large or to territory outside school property. The addressees of this policy are not fully sui juris; they are minors, or at least most of them are.[11]

Together, these two rulings questionably argue that school rules may be more vague than the criminal code due to four factors. First, they argue that the punishment of students is less severe than criminal sanctions. Although this is true, school punishment of students is still a serious matter, and it is difficult to understand why the severity of criminal sanctions justifies a lower threshold of breadth and clarity for school regulations. As the *Sullivan* court persuasively argued, basic notions of justice and fair play require that no student be punished unless standards of behavior have first been announced.[12]

Second, these rulings correctly note the hybrid character of school regulations, which pertain only to students and are confined to school property during school hours. Unfortunately, the courts fail to explain why this hybrid nature mitigates the void-for-vagueness doctrine.

Third, the courts argue that because the rules pertain to minors a higher degree of vagueness is permissible. Again, why this should be the case is not explained. In fact, if minors are to be held responsible for their actions, they ought to be sufficiently informed of the possible or probable consequences of their actions while they attend school.

Finally, these two courts find school regulations to be inevitably conceptually general. This implies that such rules are especially problematic, but the courts fail to explain this point in a convincing manner.[13]

Together, these mitigating factors fail to provide a convincing rationale for accepting overly broad and general regulations of student speech. Comparisons with the criminal code are neither helpful nor necessary. Instead, the courts ought to focus upon a "reasonable student" standard, guided by notions of justice and fair play.

A second principle regarding the proper reach of authority ought to guide school officials. The articulation requirement demands that they articulate how the goals of the school rule are related to the operation of the public school and the affected category of speech. This concern regarding the operation of the school suggests that the location of the student expression is a significant factor in determining its constitutional protection. Accordingly, student expression that originates and is distributed off school grounds should be presumed less likely to adversely affect the operation of the school. The authority of officials over student expression occurring off school premises should not be coextensive with that over student speech occurring on school premises. A federal district court explained the rationale for such a distinction in a 1969 ruling that overturned a school rule restricting the off-campus distribution of a student underground newspaper:

> In this court's judgment, it makes little sense to extend the influence of school administration to off-campus activity under the theory that such activity might interfere with the function of education. School officials may not judge a student's behavior while he is in his home with his family nor does it seem to this court that they should have jurisdiction over his acts on

> a public street corner. A student is subject to the same criminal
> laws and owes the same civil duties as other citizens, and his
> status as a student should not alter his obligations to others
> during his private life away from the campus.[14]

In other words, if school officials merit special deference because of
the important state interests they serve, then their authority must be
carefully circumscribed to those official duties. This explains, to
some extent, the logic of *Tinker's* focus on the operation of the
schools, which recognizes that the authority of school officials, like
all state agents, ought to correspond with their prescribed duties and
responsibilities. This "geographic" component accounts, in part, for
the substantial protection federal courts have afforded student underground publications. Conversely, as explained in Chapter Six, it
also serves to justify extending greater authority to officials over
school-sponsored publications.

Together, the generality principle and the reach-of-authority
principle should assist school officials in satisfying the articulation
requirement. School regulations must sufficiently articulate what
speech is restricted, what goals are served by the restriction, and
how the restricted speech pertains to the operation of the school.

Permissibility Requirement

This requirement guards against school policies that constitute
"viewpoint discrimination." Such policies restrict particular views
and opinions rather than an entire category of speech. For example,
the *Tinker* Court noted that the school officials involved did not
forbid the wearing of all symbols of political or other controversial
significance. Instead, they prohibited only black armbands worn
to protest the Vietnam War.[15] The Court forcefully stated that to
prohibit a particular opinion, at least without evidence that it is
necessary to avoid material and substantial interference with school-

work or discipline, is not constitutionally permissible.[16] The *Tinker* Court correctly warned that permitting viewpoint discrimination would encourage school officials to view students as "closed-circuit recipients" and transform our public schools into "enclaves of totalitarianism."[17]

The permissibility requirement is vital in protecting independent student speech because it demands tolerance of speech that is often savagely critical of school officials. Understandably, those criticized are prone to censor student speech based upon the views expressed. By banning viewpoint discrimination, the courts prescribe a healthy dose of tolerance that will surely taste bitter to many school authorities.

Balancing Requirement

This aspect of focused balancing demands that the state show how the regulation serves a government interest that outweighs its impact on speech. In toleration disputes, two related government interests are at stake: classroom order and the inculcative function. Thus, to satisfy the balancing requirement, school officials must convince the courts that these state interests outweigh the free-speech interests of students.

Tolerance lies at the core of every serious defense of free speech.[18] A "marketplace of ideas" requires a healthy dose of tolerance for competition.[19] Absent such tolerance, communicative expression becomes the domain of a powerful few, thereby undermining market principles. For ideas and opinions to do battle, opponents must demonstrate substantial mutual tolerance.

The democratic values served by free speech also demand substantial tolerance. Political dialogue presumes a citizenry tolerant enough to listen to opposing views.[20] Thus, robust political dialogue requires a modicum of patience, attentiveness, and self-restraint by the participants, the audience, and, of course, the government.

Similarly, the epistemic, self-realization argument demands tolerance from both state and citizens. For free speech to enhance individual self-realization and social diversity, citizens must, at the very least, tolerate religious, political, and cultural differences. Regardless of our inclination to shake our heads in dismay, disgust, or bemusement, if free speech is to serve epistemic goals, then substantial tolerance is needed to protect those whose speech and self-expression we consider to be excessively foolish, gaudy, ascetic, or extreme.

The disutility argument equates suppression with intolerance. It follows that the antidote for the ills of suppression is tolerance.[21] We ought to demonstrate our tolerance by providing those employing rebellious and radical speech a forum to vent their outrage. Such a display of tolerance provides a social safety valve, minimizing the likelihood of violence and conflict.

The incompetence argument advanced by Frederick Schauer reflects a severe distrust of the capacity of government to restrict speech.[22] This distrust rests, in some measure, on the premise that public officials are inclined not to tolerate criticism. Here, given the pervasive tug of intolerance, free speech requires the state to be tolerant. Such widespread distrust stems, in part, from the valid perception (as noted by Schauer) that public officials are substantially driven by self-interest and are therefore willing to thwart criticism of their policies and actions.[23] The substantial toleration required by the First Amendment serves as a crucial counterbalance to an intolerant, incompetent government eager to suppress speech.

Although it remains indispensable to free speech, tolerance may conflict with the government's interests in maintaining order and inculcating values. As *Tinker* made clear, when student speech substantially disrupts classroom order, school officials may rightfully be intolerant of it. Similarly, unlimited tolerance of student speech undermines the inculcative function, since tolerance may infer endorsement of values that are directly at odds with those that the school seeks to instill.

Intolerance Impulse

Why are school officials reluctant to tolerate certain forms of student expression? One reason is that they are human, and the impulse to intolerance is endemic in human behavior. As Lee Bollinger correctly points out, intolerance may stem from two distinct vantage points.[24] Firmness or certainty of belief may stoke its fires, for if one is absolutely certain of her position she often considers it unnecessary to tolerate opposing views. Similarly, she may look upon tolerance as a sign of weakness that suggests endorsement or retrenchment from her own position.

Conversely, intolerance may be practiced by one who remains uncertain of his own position, one who regards those who hold opposing views as the enemy. Just as vanity often cloaks doubts about one's appearance, those most strident about their position, and who wish to quash opposing views, often act out of insecurity (or uncertainty).

This universal impulse toward intolerance, resulting from either certainty or uncertainty of belief, reveals itself when school officials try to suppress student expression. On its own, this point is valid but unremarkable — it merely declares that school officials are human and occasionally succumb to a universal flaw. Nonetheless, public educators are especially prone to intolerance. School officials are located in hierarchical, authoritarian relationships with students.[25] They are college-educated professionals expected to perform numerous and difficult tasks. Armed with the full force of the state, often backed by parents, they exercise a great degree of authority over children. Yet, their power over students rests, in large measure, upon coercion. Public classrooms are seldom run on democratic principles. This emphasis on authority and power over the actions and conduct of children underpins professional forces that promote intolerance among educators. Although many teachers and administrators are self-declared "benevolent dictators," the benevolence is frequently suspended when students challenge or question their authority. Finally, tyranny often rears its head when well-intentioned people pursue a self-righteous moral end in a context that reinforces their authority. While John Stuart Mill clearly did not intend his views on liberty to apply in all respects to children, his warning should give us pause before we confer undue confidence and trust upon our public educators in pursuing the "best interests" of the nation's young people:

> A State which dwarfs its men, in order that they may be more docile instruments in its hands even for beneficial purposes — will find that with small men no great thing can really be accomplished; and that the perfection of machinery to which it has sacrificed everything will in the end avail it nothing, for want of the vital power which, in order that the machine might work more smoothly, it has preferred to banish.[26]

Like the professional pressures just mentioned, institutional pressures also contribute to the intolerance of public school officials. For example, being bureaucratic institutions, public schools give high priority to the pursuit of classroom order and student conformity.[27] Observers of public education are often struck by how much time and energy are expended by school officials in dictating and controlling the actions and behavior of students.[28] Formal operating procedures require passes to the lavatories, promote punctuality, discourage absences, regulate student dress, and enforce decorum in the lunchroom. This pursuit of order, discipline, and conformity is, in large measure, a response by school officials to the demands placed upon them by local citizens. As mentioned in Chapter One, Gallup polls consistently reflect the public's concern over school discipline.[29] Together, these institutional and personal pressures for order make the problem of intolerance especially acute for teachers. "Permissiveness" is one label most educators wish to avoid — for many critics of public education, tolerance becomes synonymous with permissiveness, which is seen to lie at the core of much of what ails the public schools today.[30] Justice Black forcefully expressed such a view in his *Tinker* dissent:

> Uncontrolled and uncontrollable liberty is an enemy to domestic peace. We cannot close our eyes to the fact that some of the country's greatest problems are crimes committed by the youth, too many of school age. School discipline, like parental discipline, is an integral and important part of training our children to be good citizens — to be better citizens. . . . One does not need to be a prophet or the son of a prophet to know that after the Court's holding today some students in Iowa schools and indeed in all schools will be ready, able, and willing to defy their teachers on practically all orders. This is the more unfortunate for the schools since groups of students all over the land are already running loose, conducting break-ins, sit-ins, lie-ins, and smash-ins. . . . This case, therefore, wholly without constitutional reasons in my judgment, subjects all the public schools in the country to the whims and caprices of their loudest-mouthed, but maybe not their brightest students.[31]

Student behavior significantly encourages the intolerance impulse as well. Neither the capacity of young people to defy adult authority nor their capacity to be intolerant toward each other should be underestimated. In other words, public educators are intolerant of their students because that is often the appropriate response. As Lee Bollinger explains, tolerance is not always a virtue to be applauded:

> There are times when tolerance constitutes moral weakness and is itself properly to be condemned, just as there are times when responding "intolerantly" is a sign of admirable strength — though because we usually use the term intolerance pejoratively, we express ourselves on these occasions negatively, saying we must "not tolerate" something when that is regarded as the appropriate response.[32]

Finally, because children may lack the maturity to distinguish tolerance from endorsement, they may construe tolerance as official sanction. This helps us understand why educators refuse to tolerate student speech. For both educators and the general public, toleration often becomes synonymous with weakness. School officials do not appreciate being perceived as weak-willed adults incapable of controlling children, and they frequently respond in intolerant fashion. The balancing requirement compels them to exercise a healthy dose of self-restraint.

Tolerance, Inculcation, and Order

While unlimited tolerance of independent student speech may threaten state interests, a substantial degree of tolerance may serve classroom order and the inculcative function in a number of ways. If tolerance conveys respect for students, the moral authority of school officials is enhanced. In addition, due to limited time and resources, school officials cannot possibly confront and correct all student behavior that offends their sensibilities or entails violations of school rules; educators, like other authorities, must choose their battles carefully. Thus, tolerating some student speech, especially that which does not significantly threaten classroom order, allows officials to direct greater effort toward more pressing dangers, such as student violence.

Social integration into a liberal, pluralistic society requires both the state and the citizenry to be sufficiently tolerant.[33] Tolerance, then, is important to the inculcative function for the role it plays in advancing social change. For example, public schools are responsible for integrating immigrants, racial minorities, and disabled citizens.[34] Accordingly, school officials are expected to simultaneously tolerate a diverse student body and develop a tolerant student body. The inculcative function is not merely concerned with maintaining and transmitting existing shared community values. It may also entail changing and transforming social values and attitudes about race, gender, and class. To develop a diverse, harmonious student body successfully, school officials need to inculcate tolerance.

Educators, then, ought to consider tolerance to be both a value to inculcate and an effective inculcative strategy. Along with parents and judges, they argue that school officials (especially teachers) often serve as role models for students.[35] If toleration is a key inculcative value, it makes sense for school officials to practice it. Educators who expect students to treat each other with respect and dignity will be more successful if they practice what they preach.

Limits of Tolerance

The courts should require school officials to tolerate independent student speech that does not violate the *Tinker* disruption standard. Educators should not, however, be forced to be neutral or passive toward student utterance. They can respond to and even attack independent student speech in a nonpunitive manner. For example, the *Tinker* students were not seeking official assistance, nor did they expect school officials to be indifferent or neutral toward what they were doing. Indeed, it can be argued that the students wore the armbands to draw attention to their antiwar views and did not want school officials to "turn their heads."

Although there is a solid case for tolerating independent student speech, in certain situations the state's interests outweigh the First Amendment rights of students. The substantial-disruption standard set forth in *Tinker* correctly recognizes the right of school officials to restrict speech that undermines classroom order. Similarly, the inculcative function supersedes the First Amendment rights of students in two contexts. First, it may justify restricting "offensive" or "vulgar" student expression. School officials should not be presumptively required to tolerate such expression, regardless of its visible impact on classroom order. In 1979, a federal appellate judge explained the rationale for leaving offensive student speech unprotected. In a ruling concerned with the distribution and publication of a student underground newspaper, a concurring Judge Newman declared that student free speech should not be coextensive with that of adults, due to the special nature of public schools:

School authorities can regulate indecent language because its circulation on school grounds undermines their responsibility to try to promote standards of decency and civility among school children. The task may be difficult, perhaps unlikely ever to be more than marginally successful. But whether a school condemns or tolerates indecent language within its sphere of authority will have significance for the future of that school and of its students. The First Amendment does not prevent a school's reasonable efforts toward the maintenance of campus standards of civility and decency. With its captive audience of children, many of whom, along with their parents, legitimately expect reasonable regulation, a school need not capitulate to a student's preference for vulgar expression. A school's authority to condemn indecent language is not inconsistent with a student's right to express his views. In short, the First Amendment gives a high school student the classroom right to wear Tinker's armband, but not Cohen's jacket.[36]

Paul Cohen had entered a courthouse in Los Angeles in 1968 wearing a jacket with the words Fuck the Draft on the back. The United States Supreme Court declared such expression to be protected by the First Amendment.[37] Forbidding Cohen's jacket on school grounds makes abundant sense, for, unlike the courtroom, a classroom entails a captive audience of young people.

Distinguishing adult expression inside a courthouse from student speech on school grounds requires caution, however, for school officials may squelch legitimate expression under the guise of merely regulating indecent, offensive speech. For example, an underground newspaper typically includes political and social commentary, often satirical, as well as blatantly offensive and vulgar speech. *Grass High,* one such student newspaper, contained the random remark, "Oral sex may prevent tooth decay." For this and other reasons, school officials sought to restrict the distribution of the newspaper. A federal district court ruled that their actions violated the First Amendment, suggesting that their sensitivity and outrage over such remarks resulted from a "generation gap."[38] In *Cohen*, the Supreme Court declared that "one man's vulgarity is another's lyric."[39] Perhaps this is especially true in regard to different generations.

Another case also demonstrates a significant departure from the *Tinker* rule, and similarly illustrates a context in which the inculcative function supersedes student free-speech interests. In *Williams v. Spencer*, the Fourth Circuit Court of Appeals upheld a school regulation that permitted administrators to halt the distribution of any student publication that encouraged actions which endangered the health or safety of students.[40] School officials had confiscated copies of a student underground newspaper that contained an advertisement for a store that specialized in the sale of drug paraphernalia. The advertisement promoted the sale of a water pipe used to smoke marijuana and hashish, along with paraphernalia used in connection with cocaine. The court rejected the students' argument that the school rule was impermissibly vague and thus violated the First Amendment.[41] The Fourth Circuit Court of Appeals did hold, however, that disruption is merely one justification for school authorities to restrain the distribution of a publication; nowhere has it been held to be the sole justification.[42] Here, the interest of the school in seeing that materials which encourage actions that endanger the health or safety of students are not distributed on school property supersedes the First Amendment rights of students.[43]

This broad reading of *Tinker* is proper, especially considering that the advertisement encouraged criminal behavior. The potential or likely disruption that might result from the advertisement should not decide its permissibility. Given the nature and character of the advertisement, the possibility or probability of disruption should not constrain school officials.

Conclusion

Focused balancing seems helpful and appropriate for resolving First Amendment disputes over independent student expression that is not sponsored by a school. The articulation requirement demands that administrators be sufficiently precise in forging school policies restricting student speech. A "reasonable student" should understand what expression is forbidden, the procedures by which the policies operate, and the probable sanctions for violating the rules. The permissibility requirement serves notice to school officials that viewpoint discrimination, when detected, will make such policies presumptively invalid. The balancing requirement limits, but does not quash, student speech, for it properly weighs legitimate government interests against the aims of the First Amendment. Together, a level of judicial review emerges that confers a significant measure of First Amendment protection for independent student speech. We shall now see how well focused balancing resolves disputes involving student speech that requires the assistance or association of public schools.

Six

Assisting Student Expression

[Educators] do not offend the First

Amendment by exercising editorial control

over the style and content of student speech

in school-sponsored expressive activities so

> long as their actions are reasonably related
>
> to legitimate pedagogical concerns.
>
> *Hazelwood School District v. Kuhlmeier*

Students frequently ask school officials for three kinds of assistance in promoting their ideas and beliefs: funding, faculty supervision, and access to school facilities. Fearing that such assistance associates the school system with controversial, distasteful student speech, school officials deny many of these requests. When they do grant them, administrators usually try to control the content and character of the student speech. Not surprisingly, their efforts occasionally fuel First Amendment litigation.

The distinction between officials tolerating and assisting independent student speech is imprecise. Nonetheless, requiring school officials to tolerate *Tinker* armbands is different from requiring them to supervise or fund a "student coalition for peace."[1] As noted in a 1988 Supreme Court ruling, it is one thing for the courts to tell school officials that they must tolerate independent student expression, but quite another to say that they must provide affirmative assistance for student speech.[2]

Public Forums and Public Schools

School policies and practices regarding association are hybrid restrictions, for they are typically content based and they apply only to particular locations or specific speakers.[3] The courts have increasingly employed public forum analysis for association disputes.[4] Unfortunately, this doctrinal approach has not produced a coherent framework for addressing the key issues and concerns raised in such litigation. On the one hand, federal courts suggest that public forum analysis is seductively straightforward. For example, in *Gambino v. Fairfax City School Board,* a high school principal censored an article entitled "Sexually Active Students Fail to Use Contraception."[5] The federal district court reduced the case to one controlling issue: Is the school-sponsored student newspaper a protected public forum? If the answer is yes, then the article receives First Amendment protection. If the answer is no, then the actions of the school officials need only meet a "reasonableness standard."[6] Here, the court found the paper to be a protected designated public forum.[7]

Such straightforward framing of the issues is misleading, for public forum analysis actually entails four related inquiries.[8] First, the court must decide if school officials have created a limited public forum. Next, if such a forum has been established, the court must determine if the First Amendment protects the proposed student activity. Third, if the activity is protected, the court must then apply strict scrutiny and determine if the state has a compelling interest and if its actions are closely tailored. Finally, if a limited public forum is not found, or if the proposed activity falls outside a limited forum's parameter, the issue before the court is merely whether the restrictions have a rational basis and do not constitute impermissible viewpoint discrimination.

Not surprisingly, the courts struggle with each of these inquiries. To determine if a public forum has been created, the courts must discern the intent of school officials. Although examining the written record and past practices aids in this effort, school boards, like other deliberative bodies, often have multiple purposes and motivations for their actions.

Because a public school often includes stadiums, gymnasiums, and auditoriums as well as classrooms, public forum analysis leads the courts into a judicial thicket. For example, in *Student Coalition for Peace v. Lower Merion School District,* a student organization sought to have a "peace exposition" on school grounds.[9] They requested the use of the athletic stadium, the athletic field, the courtyard, and the boys' gymnasium. To determine the forum status of the school, the federal district court examined the past activities permitted on each site.[10] Such judicial gymnastics dispel the notion that public forum analysis entails a straightforward inquiry.

Public forum analysis for associative disputes yields inconsistent rulings. For example, the courts have employed two conflicting standards for determining whether a school-sponsored student newspaper is a limited public forum. In *Gambino v. Fairfax City School Board,* the federal district court stated that, if the school-sponsored student newspaper was established as a vehicle for expression, it constituted a limited public forum.[11] This standard ensures a particular outcome, since a student newspaper, like every newspaper, is a "vehicle for expression" and thus becomes a limited public forum.

In *Hazelwood School District v. Kuhlmeier,* the United States Supreme Court imposed a different standard that makes it more difficult to transform a school-sponsored newspaper into a limited public forum.[12] Here, a public forum exists only when school facilities have been opened for "indiscriminate use" by the general public or by some segment of it, such as student organizations. However, if facilities have been reserved for other intended purposes, "communicative or otherwise," then no public forum has been created and officials may then impose reasonable restrictions.[13] This standard makes it unlikely that a court will declare a school-sponsored student newspaper to be a limited public forum, since even the most tolerant school officials are not likely to support the "indiscriminate use" of a student newspaper for the general public.

These two judicial approaches produce conflicting outcomes, for the *Gambino* standard guarantees broad First Amendment protection for student publications, while the one in *Hazelwood* protects the student press more narrowly. Thus, public forum analysis requires judges to find either a "limited public forum," thereby triggering a stringent level of review, or to find no public forum, thereby applying a lenient "reasonableness standard." In place of these polarized levels of review, a more coherent, intermediate level of judicial scrutiny is needed for resolving associative disputes.

Articulation Requirement

Focused balancing's articulation requirement imposes four related tasks upon school officials. First, the school policy must explain the criteria for distinguishing independent student expression from associative speech. Thus, it must identify the point at which funding, supervision, or access to facilities constitutes "association."

Second, school officials must articulate the procedures for the process of reviewing student speech. Authorities must adequately notify students of the steps necessary to submit their requests for school facilities or to present their publications for prior approval.[14]

In addition, school officials must specify the aims of the policy. For example, if one goal is to preserve classroom order, then the authorities must adequately define what constitutes impermissible disruption. Similarly, if the policy serves "pedagogical interests" or the "inculcative function," it must satisfactorily explain the content of such goals.

Finally, school officials need to explain how the procedures and sanctions serve the stated goals of the policy. For example, they must demonstrate how censoring an article or denying a request to use school facilities serves the inculcative function. Thus, to satisfy the articulation requirement, a school policy must set out the affected category of speech, the particular procedures of the policy, its stated goals, and how the policy's means are related to its ends.

How precise and specific must school regulations be? Over the past two decades, the federal courts have proposed various guidelines, some more helpful than others. One federal district court, addressing a dispute regarding censorship of a student yearbook, declared that censorial regulations must be "reasonably precise and ascertainable."[15] Similarly, after examining a school regulation that acted as a prior restraint on the distribution of pamphlets not sponsored by the school, the Fourth Circuit Court of Appeals stated that such a policy must contain "narrow, objective, and reasonable" standards.[16] In striking down a ban on the distribution of underground newspapers on school grounds, federal appeals court merely conceded that the regulation need not be as exacting as the criminal code.[17] On occasion, federal courts have declared certain linguistic terms to be insufficiently precise and clear. Thus, the Fourth Circuit Court of Appeals found a school regulation addressing "libelous" and "obscene" speech to be impermissibly vague.[18] Similarly, a federal district court found standards of "taste" and "appropriateness" to be impermissible, for they were completely subjective.[19]

These judicial standards reflect, in part, the problems stemming from the inherent ambiguity of language. Standards governing libel, obscenity, taste, and appropriateness have no fixed meaning.[20] However, judicial dictates may be as ambiguous as the school rules frequently struck down by the courts. For example, the *Tinker* standard regarding "material disruption" is not necessarily precise or clear. While it may be proper in spirit for a court to declare that a school regulation must be "narrow, objective, and reasonable," such a standard is no more precise than a school regulation that restricts "offensive" or "vulgar" speech.

Undoubtedly, an excessively vague and unclear school policy grants officials an all-encompassing authority to restrict student speech, thereby establishing the "enclaves of totalitarianism" that *Tinker* properly sought to prohibit. Justice William J. Brennan warned of such a danger in his scathing dissent in *Hazelwood School District v. Kuhlmeier*:

> Free student expression undoubtedly sometimes interferes with the effectiveness of the school's pedagogical functions. . . . If mere incompatability with the school's pedagogical message were a constitutionally sufficient justification for the suppression of student speech, school officials could censor each of the students or student organizations in the foregoing hypotheticals, converting our public schools into "enclaves of totalitarianism," . . . that "strangle the free mind at its source." . . . The First Amendment permits no such blanket censorship authority.[21]

Conversely, by demanding a high degree of precision, the courts may interfere excessively with the legitimate authority of school officials. For example, after scrutinizing a rule pertaining to independent student newspapers, one court deemed such terms as "pupil days" and "submit" to be impermissibly vague.[22] Such rulings do little to provide guidance for school officials. Rather, they reflect both the courts' willingness to play a negative role that says "not good enough" and their reluctance (or inability) to assist school officials in forging language that is more precise and clear. In sum, the courts' proposed cures are seldom an improvement.

Given the problems of ambiguity facing both school officials and federal judges, perhaps the best the courts can do is to demand that school rules be "reasonable" and "fair." By employing a "reasonable student" standard, the courts secure adequate notice for students. Such a device provides the courts with a flexible, heuristic standard to help ensure that school policies are sufficiently precise. In this way, a typical student can understand what speech is restricted, what procedures to follow, and what sanctions may be imposed if she violates the policy. Justice Thurgood Marshall explains:

> It is . . . essential that legislation aimed at protecting children from allegedly harmful expression — no less than legislation enacted with respect to adults — be clearly drawn and that the standards adopted be reasonably precise so that those who are governed by the law and those that administer it will understand its meaning and application.[23]

Accordingly, adequate procedural safeguards require that school regulations and policies be in writing and be made available to students. The Supreme Court has recognized that public education is a protected property interest, and that students must be notified of the consequences of their speech.[24] Thus, written policies are best suited for providing a "reasonable student" adequate notice regarding the consequences of her speech.

Together, the "reasonable" and "fairness" principles impose an intermediate level of scrutiny that falls between the rigorous strict-scrutiny standard of review and the boilerplate rationality test. Thus, this intermediate level of judicial scrutiny would be neither insurmountable nor pro forma.[25]

Permissibility Requirement

This element of focused balancing forbids school officials from restricting speech based on the specific views being expressed. For several reasons, this presumptive ban on viewpoint discrimination is ill-suited for associative disputes. First, the problem is often difficult to detect. A 1988 Supreme Court decision, *Hazelwood School District v. Kuhlmeier,* illustrates the difficulty.[26] Here, a high school principal, concerned about two articles, censored a portion of the school-sponsored student newspaper. One article discussed pregnancy among fellow students, while the other interviewed students who were children of divorced parents. In a five to three ruling, the Court did not find the principal's actions to constitute viewpoint discrimination. It concluded, rather, that the principal acted reasonably in censoring articles dealing with "sensitive topics."[27]

A dissenting Justice Brennan, however, saw the actions in a quite different light: "The case before us aptly illustrates how readily school officials (and courts) can camouflage viewpoint discrimination as the 'mere' protection of students from sensitive topics."[28] These conflicting assessments of the principal's actions remind us that the views expressed may be inseparable from the content. In the case of the censored article that dealt with divorce, one student (originally identified by name) complained that her father "wasn't spending enough time with my mom, my sister and I" and "was always out of town on business or out late playing cards with the guys."[29] According to the principal, he censored the article because the student's father should have been given an opportunity to respond to the remarks or to consent to their publication. Was the principal engaged in viewpoint discrimination? The answer is not obvious — and this is the point. Had the article not been so candid in its criticism of parents, it would have slighted the impact of divorce upon students. Thus, the daughter's criticism (or viewpoint) of her father was integral to, and perhaps even inseparable from, the content or topic of the article.

Applying a stringent permissibility requirement to associative disputes is at odds with legitimate viewpoint discrimination. To fulfill their duties and responsibilities, including the inculcative function, public educators may properly refuse to assist certain views. In other words, school officials ought to have greater authority to restrict student utterance that receives the imprimatur of the school than they enjoy in restricting independent student expression. What school officials must tolerate, they need not endorse. Thus, the views that they must tolerate in underground student papers need not be permitted in a newspaper sponsored by the school. Administrators should have the discretionary authority to withhold their assistance in disseminating or their endorsement of positions that are contrary to their duties and responsibilities.

The following hypothetical scenario illustrates why viewpoint discrimination should be permitted for associative student speech. Student journalists at Midtown High School, for a school-sponsored newspaper, wrote a series of profiles of "Great Americans" that included Abraham Lincoln, Martin Luther King, Jr., and Hugh Hefner. Although the articles were informative and well-written, the school authorities were uncomfortable associating the school with an article singing the praises of Hefner, the publisher of *Playboy*. Does the First Amendment require administrators to permit publication of each article? The point is not whether the officials should allow the Hefner article to be published in the school newspaper; a strong case can be made that they should. What is at issue is whether the federal courts should conclude that the First Amendment requires school authorities to publish the article. Certainly, the officials practice viewpoint discrimination if they censor the Hefner article. Nonetheless, administrators should be allowed to restrict the article, regardless of whether it leads to the level of disruption established in *Tinker*. School officials ought to be allowed considerable (not unlimited) authority to place parameters on associative student expression.

Similarly, viewpoint discrimination ought to be allowed when students request official recognition of their organizations. If officials recognize Young Republicans and Young Democrats, must they also sanction Young Socialists, Young Anarchists, and Young Klansmen? Similarly, if officials recognize a student ecology club or business club, must they also countenance an animal rights group, a gay and lesbian support group, or an anti–secular humanism club? Certainly, one can argue the pedagogical benefits of granting recognition to all of these groups. What is at issue, however, is not whether school officials should honor such requests, but whether the First Amendment requires them to grant official recognition to each request.

By presumptively forbidding viewpoint discrimination, the permissibility requirement imposes an undue burden upon school officials. Viewpoint discrimination remains difficult to discern, and it is often both necessary and desirable in certain circumstances. Thus, this requirement seems inappropriate for associative disputes.

Balancing Requirement

Under this aspect of focused balancing, school officials must show that the governmental interest served by a restriction outweighs its impact on student speech. To properly balance state interests against the First Amendment rights of public school students, the courts must use a "thumb-on-the-scales" approach. Judges, in other words, ought to take infringement of student expression seriously.

Censoring specific articles has a dramatic impact upon student speech, as do prior-approval policies for their publications. Similarly, withholding recognition of organizations may infringe upon student expression. However, the impact upon student speech is tempered by the hybrid character of school restrictions. When officials censor articles or deny recognition to groups, they close off two avenues of student expression, but not all — such alternatives as underground newspapers and private associations remain available. In addition, the inculcative function serves as a counterbalance to First Amendment interests. In *Bethel School District No. 403 v. Fraser,* the United States Supreme Court explains:

> These fundamental values of "habits and manners of civility" essential to a democratic society must, of course, include tolerance of divergent political and religious views, even when the views expressed may be unpopular. But these "fundamental values" must also take into account consideration of the sensibilities of others, and, in the case of a school, the sensibilities of fellow students. The undoubted freedom to advocate unpopular and controversial views in schools and classrooms must be balanced against the society's countervailing interest in teaching students the boundaries of socially appropriate behavior.[30]

In resolving disputes over associative student speech, we must consider more than the *Tinker* disruption standard when weighing the government interest against the impact on student speech. Disruption of the classroom is not always observable, for it may take forms other than the purely physical.[31] Children may be made quite upset by the speech of fellow students, yet fail to convey their emotions in a demonstrative or disruptive manner. Fear, anger, resentment, revulsion, or embarrassment may explain the veneer of passive acquiescence, making student speech disruptive in ways not easily observable. Of course, invisible disruption may serve as a ruse for school officials to justify any speech restriction, and *Tinker* correctly requires them to base their actions on more than "undifferentiated fear." Although the *Tinker* disruption standard has considerable merit, it should not be the sole or decisive guide for resolving all student speech disputes.

Judicial fixation on *Tinker* misconstrues the complexities of student free-speech disputes. While the disruption standard has considerable force with regard to toleration cases, for cases involving association it must be viewed as only one of several grounds for censorship. Even when student expression is not disruptive, schools do not need to offer it official endorsement or assistance. This kind of utterance may well be met with silence or indifference by the student body. But such a response does not necessarily legitimate the speech, nor does it require school officials to "associate" with it.

Bethel v. Fraser

In a 1986 ruling, the Supreme Court recognized that the *Tinker* disruption standard is not the only justification for censoring student speech. Matthew Fraser, a high school student in Bethel, Washington, gave the following nominating speech at a school assembly in April 1983:

> I know a man who is firm — he's firm in his pants, he's firm in his shirt, his character is firm — but most of all, his belief in you, the student of Bethel is firm. Jeff Kuhlman is a man who takes his point and pounds it in. If necessary, he'll take an issue and nail it to the wall — He doesn't attack things in spurts — he drives hard, pushing and pushing until finally — he succeeds.
>
> Jeff is a man who will go to the very end — even the climax, for each and every one of you. So vote for Jeff for ASB vice president — he'll never come between you and the best our high school can be.[32]

Not surprisingly, school authorities did not appreciate Fraser's speech; they suspended him for three days and removed his name from a list of potential commencement speakers. Fraser, in turn, brought suit in federal court, charging that the school's actions violated the First Amendment, along with the due process clause of the Fourteenth Amendment. He sought both injunctive relief and monetary damages.

The district court agreed with Fraser, finding that the school's actions violated the First and Fourteenth Amendments. The court of appeals affirmed the judgment of the district court.[33] The United States Supreme Court, in a seven to two ruling, reversed, finding no violation of either amendment.[34]

Writing for the majority, Chief Justice Warren Burger argued that even *Tinker* did not protect "offensive" speech; nor did *Tinker* protect speech that is "materially disruptive."[35] Fraser's speech, according to Burger, was both offensive and disruptive, and thereby not protected by the First Amendment. In addition, the Court recognized the importance of the inculcative function and the fact that educators serve as role models for students.

> The schools, as instruments of the state, may determine that the essential lessons of civil, mature conduct cannot be conveyed in a school that tolerates, lewd, indecent, or offensive speech and conduct such as that indulged in by this confused boy. . . . A high school assembly or classroom is no place for a sexually explicit monologue directed towards an unsuspecting audience of teenage students. Accordingly, it was perfectly appropriate for the school to disassociate itself to make the point to the pupils that vulgar speech and lewd conduct is wholly inconsistent with the "fundamental values" of public school education.[36]

The majority also concluded that the school rule did not violate Fraser's right to due process, for the regulation upon which the suspension rested gave sufficient notice to Fraser, and school rules need not be as rigid as a criminal code.[37]

Hazelwood v. Kuhlmeier

In a 1988 ruling, the Supreme Court again recognized other grounds for censorship besides the disruption standard. In May 1983 a high school journalism class in St. Louis County, Missouri, sought to include two articles in the final issue of their school newspaper. One discussed teenage pregnancy, while the other addressed the impact of divorce on high school students. After reviewing the entire newspaper prior to publication, the principal of Hazelwood High School, disturbed by the nature and content of these two articles, censored them by excising two full pages of the newspaper.

Three students on the staff brought suit against the school district, seeking a declaration that the principal's action violated their First Amendment rights. They sought both injunctive relief and monetary damages. The federal district court, employing a "reasonable standard" test, denied the injunction.[38] The court of appeals reversed, finding the principal's actions unreasonable and thereby violative of the First Amendment.[39]

The United States Supreme Court, in a five to three decision, reversed, holding that the principal's actions did not violate the First Amendment. Writing for the majority, Justice Byron White argued that, given the special characteristics of public schools, school newspapers are not always public forums, and therefore they deserve less protection than is generally accorded other print publications.[40]

The Court also articulated a new standard to replace the "material disruption" standard created in *Tinker.* The Court declared that educators exercising editorial control over the content and style of student speech in school-sponsored expressive activities do not violate the First Amendment "so long as their actions are reasonably related to legitimate pedagogical concerns."[41]

Drawing upon *Fraser,* the majority granted school authorities the right to refuse to sponsor student speech inconsistent with "the shared values of a civilized social order."[42] Without such authority, the Court maintained, schools would be unduly restrained from fulfilling their role in awakening students to cultural values.[43] Thus, the majority concluded that disruption was not the sole justification for censoring school-sponsored newspapers.[44] The Court distinguished *Tinker* from the case at hand by noting that in *Tinker* a school sought to punish independent student expression, while in this case the school merely refused to lend its name and resources to the dissemination of student expression. Accordingly, the majority granted greater discretion to officials who want to dissociate the school from certain student speech.[45] The majority considered this stance to be consistent with local governance of public education.

A dissenting Justice Brennan found the Court's ruling to be a tragic retreat from the standards and principles established in *Tinker*:[46] "Tinker teaches us that the state educator's undeniable, and undeniably vital, mandate to inculcate moral and political values is not a general warrant to act as 'thought police' stifling discussion of all but state-approved topics and advocacy of all but the official position."[47] Finding the principal's actions unreasonable, Brennan condemned him for using a "paper shredder" when a more sensitive tool was needed. In a sharp rebuke, the justice stated that such unthinking contempt for individual rights is intolerable from any state official.[48] Brennan also rejected the majority's distinction between tolerance and association.[49] Such a retreat by the Court, he argued, effectively "denudes" students of whatever constitutional "clothing" *Tinker* provided them beyond the schoolhouse gate.[50]

Weighing the Inculcative Function

The *Fraser* and *Hazelwood* rulings recognize the limited utility of the *Tinker* disruption standard for associative disputes. Both decisions give sufficient weight to the inculcative function, and both imply that protection of a student audience may supersede the autonomy of student speakers.[51]

The inculcative function and the association distinction are closely related, for both recognize that school officials have a special duty to model the values they want to instill in students. Thus, federal courts should distinguish independent student expression from speech that bears the imprimatur of the school. The following case illustrates the need for this distinction.

In *Augustus v. Escambia*, students who objected to administrators' ban on using "Rebels" as the school symbol along with the

Confederate battle flag brought a suit against the school district.[52] Officials, in justifying the ban, noted that interracial disturbances had occurred in the school and that the symbol had exacerbated racial tensions among students.[53] The federal district court identified two key elements of the dispute:

> This case involves two factually related but legally distinct issues. The first consists of the effects from the use of the symbols by the school as its officially approved designation. The second concerns the effects of the private use of the symbols by students in the school environment. This distinction must be made because the law separates state encouraged discrimination from purely private discrimination.[54]

The court found that official use of the name "Rebels" and the use of the Confederate flag "seriously interfered with the effective operation of the school.[55] However, with regard to private use of the symbols by individual students while on school premises, "any limitation placed on private speech must be based on more than the speech's discriminating content."[56] The court then upheld the officials' actions, finding that even the private use of such symbols impermissibly disrupted the operation of the school, thereby violating the standard established in *Tinker.*

This ruling properly noted that the dispute entailed both First Amendment issues and Fourteenth Amendment equal protection concerns regarding racial discrimination. By applying the *Tinker* disruption standard, the court made the state's action even more legitimate. However, the court's distinction between private and state action should be decisive even if the school symbols had not exacerbated racial tensions. Certainly, the school should not be bound by the First Amendment to yield to a majority of students' demands regarding the official school symbol. Even if all of the students had wished to use the "Rebel" symbol, administrators should still be allowed to prohibit such an official symbol. Public educators have a duty to lead students, not merely respond to their demands—otherwise, the inculcative function would lose much of its force and purpose. However, if individual students wish to wear or display the "Rebel" symbol, or place a replica of the Confederate flag on their class notebook, absent a "substantial and material" disruption the school officials must tolerate such expression. This is the basis of the distinction between the toleration category and the association category. School officials must, in certain contexts, permit the private display of such symbols, but the First Amendment should not require them to give official approval to any symbol that students desire.

The balancing requirement for association disputes should note a key distinction between those pertaining to student publications and those concerning student requests for the use of school facilities. This distinction recognizes that school-sponsored publications entail a greater degree of association, for they typically involve all three associative elements — funding, supervision, and use of facilities.

Conversely, granting access to school facilities lies closer to the tolerance requests addressed in Chapter Five. Access requests are less likely to be disruptive, for they typically involve activities that take place outside regular school hours. Granting such requests usually involves less endorsement or assistance by school authorities, for they do not necessarily entail funding or faculty supervision. Accordingly, the procedures regarding such requests must be fair and reasonable. Judicial scrutiny ought to impose a significant burden of proof upon school officials to demonstrate that their actions were not based on "undifferentiated fears." The point here is that such requests, because they involve a modicum of association, permit educators to exercise greater control than was granted in the toleration categories. As the degree of association increases, however, so should the discretionary authority of school officials.

In *Fraser*, the Supreme Court correctly recognized that public education involves more than curricular decisions:

> The process of educating our youth for citizenship in public schools is not confined to books, the curriculum, and the civics class; schools must teach by example the shared values of a

> civilized social order. Consciously or otherwise, teachers — and indeed the older students — demonstrate the appropriate form of civil discourse and political expression by their conduct and deportment in and out of class. Inescapably, like parents, they are role models.[57]

Unfortunately, courts occasionally engage in tortured arguments regarding the curricular status of student publications. In *Frasca v. Andrews,* a case involving a principal's confiscation of the student newspaper, a federal district court declared the school-sponsored publication to be an "extra-curricular" activity, even though there was a faculty adviser and it was funded entirely by the local school district, which provided space, utilities, supplies, desks, typewriters, and printing.[58] In addition, some students on the newspaper staff received academic credit, and the publication was distributed in homerooms during school hours.[59]

Why is the curricular distinction important to the public forum analysis? The courts correctly understand that school curriculums cannot be rightly declared a designated public forum; curricular decisions invariably entail exclusion of ideas, thereby undermining the notion of public schools serving as "academic marketplaces." A lower federal court explains:

> A corollary of the finding that the paper "was established as a vehicle for First Amendment expression and not as an official publication is that the newspaper cannot be construed objectively as an integral part of the curriculum. . . . Therefore, because the newspaper is not in reality a part of the curriculum of the school, and because it is entitled to First Amendment protection, the power of the School Board to regulate course content will not support its action in this case."[60]

The presumption that school officials enjoy greater discretion regarding curricular decisions is even acknowledged by Justice Brennan in his *Hazelwood* dissent.[61] Because administrators have less authority to censor student speech in designated public forums than they enjoy with regard to curricular decisions, the courts must decide the curricular status of school-sponsored newspapers. If a student newspaper is a curricular activity, it is subject to greater censorial control by school officials; if it is declared a public forum, officials have less censorial authority. Thus, in *Hazelwood* the Supreme Court declared the student newspaper to be an integral part of the curriculum, due in large part to the degree of association.[62] Determining curricular status should not be decisive in associative disputes, for both association and inculcation transcend the school curriculum. With regard to school-sponsored student newspapers, the association is considerable, and the school should enjoy broad authority to disassociate itself from the student expression at issue. Disassociation can be accomplished in various ways, including disclaimers of endorsement, offering counterarguments, and outright censorship. By and large, judges should defer to school officials on deciding the most appropriate and effective means of disassociation.

Furthermore, the inculcative function is served by an array of school-sponsored activities that take place outside the classroom. Enforcing student decorum at public events, instilling notions of sportsmanship among student athletes, promoting self-discipline and confidence among student musicians and artists, all serve to inculcate important social and moral values. Accordingly, determining the forum status or the curricular status of a student newspaper misconstrues the values and interests that ought to be weighed in associative disputes concerning student expression.

Associative Student Speech

Stanton v. Brunswick provides an excellent opportunity to reflect on the various issues and concerns addressed throughout this chapter. In this case, a local school board refused to publish a quotation selected by Joellen Stanton (a graduating senior) for the high school yearbook.[63] For several years, students about to graduate had submitted quotes to be published in the yearbook, along with other personal information to be inserted next to their individual pictures. Ms. Stanton requested the following quote, which had appeared in *Time* magazine: "The executioner will pull this lever four times. Each time 2000 volts will course through your body, making your eyeballs first bulge, then burst, and then broiling your brains."[64] Ms. Stanton gave this explanation for her selection:

> The reason I chose the quotation I selected was to possibly provoke some of my classmates to think a little more deeply than if I had written a standard butterfly quote. I wanted to make them aware of the realities that exist in today's world. The issue isn't that of capital punishment alone, but of those realities of which [*sic*] people prefer to avoid. It is important to think about these things because we are seniors and we are going to be on our own very soon.[65]

Administrators told her that because the school published the yearbook it could decide its content.[66] Despite the pleas of faculty advisers, the student editor-in-chief, and the high school principal, who all agreed that the quotation was in poor taste and inappropriate for publication in the yearbook, Ms. Stanton declined to change her mind. She argued that previous yearbooks contained quotes that encouraged the use of illegal drugs and alcohol, comments from musicians that glorified sexual activity, and quotations reflecting the views of such diverse individuals as Bertolt Brecht and John F. Kennedy.[67] Subsequently, she brought suit, claiming that past practices had established a de facto public forum.

The federal district court agreed, noting the serious stakes involved in what, at first glance, others might deem a trivial case. The court took a "thumb-on-the-scales" approach, due to the inadequacy of the school policy and criteria used to justify the censorship.

> In the legitimate exercise of her right of free speech, this Plaintiff has the option to convey her conviction by the use of the

most graphic language, even, if she so chooses, by language so physiologically stark that others may believe her to "be a jerk." . . . Government has no legitimate nor compelling interest in preserving this lone woman from that fate if her own utterances shall visit it upon her. Rather, the First Amendment declares that the highest interest of the people is best served if government is required to stay its hand and permit her, and millions like her, to take upon their personal risk the ability of their ideas and convictions to survive and propagate in the marketplace of ideas. It is a matter of little moment, in the larger sense, whether she fails in that endeavor; it is of vital moment that she and her idea not be denied, by the instrumentalities of the political establishment, the opportunity to succeed in that marketplace. It is, indeed, of paramount importance to the public interest that she have that opportunity.[68]

According to the court, "taste" was not a sufficient standard, for the emotive content of expression cannot be sacrificed to arbitrary official standards of taste.[69]

The impact upon student speech in this case was significant, but not severe. Alternative avenues were available through which Ms. Stanton could express her sentiments regarding capital punishment. The school officials did not forbid her from expressing her views by speaking to others. She could have made her position quite public by writing a letter to the editor of the school newspaper, or, for a wider audience, to the local newspaper. Indeed, she could have personally written the same message when asked to write in her fellow students' yearbooks, as is often the custom for graduating seniors. In fact, she would have been allowed to express her disapproval of the death penalty in language more acceptable to the school officials and the student editor. While the availability of alternative avenues is not decisive regarding adult First Amendment rights, it ought to carry more weight in this context, since the rights of students are not coextensive with those of adults.

In addition, the impact on student speech is tempered, since the sanctions imposed by the school officials were less likely to have a chilling effect upon protected speech. With notable exceptions such as *Fraser,* censorial authority regarding associative cases rarely involves such harsh disciplinary measures as school suspensions. The punishment inflicted on Ms. Stanton was merely the withdrawal of assistance in airing her views, and this significant (but not severe) sanction is not likely to have a substantial chilling effect.

Since the importance of the inculcative function parallels the degree of association, we should consider the degree of association at issue with Ms. Stanton's yearbook quotation. Because faculty members supervised the yearbook, the court concluded that its preparation and publication was an integral part of the general program of secondary education.[70] On the other hand, the character of the quote was clearly personal, and association of the school with it was, at most, indirect, since the context made it clear that Ms. Stanton, and not the school officials, had made the selection. The association stemmed from the fact that it appeared at all, and the school could have put a disclaimer in the yearbook explicitly disassociating itself from any of the quotes.[71]

This case also demonstrates specific flaws of public forum analysis. The court's notion that a yearbook ought to be regarded as a "marketplace of ideas" is especially misguided. The array of legitimate exceptions to what school officials must allow is so numerous as to make the marketplace notion hollow. Certainly the court should allow officials to exclude quotations that are vulgar, but not necessarily obscene, such as "Eat Shit!" But what about "Dixie Forever!"; "Abortion Is Murder!"; "Jesus Saves!"; "Condoms Are Cool!" Which, if any, of these examples should be deemed protected speech? Reasonable arguments can be made to permit or censor each statement. The question at hand is to what extent the First Amendment prevents school officials from making the decision to allow such statements in a school-sponsored publication.

Another ill stemming from public forum analysis is that it permits the past to shape the present. Thus, past errors in judgment may rightfully demand remedial action by school officials who wish to declare "No More!" These sorts of abrupt changes in school policy may be invidious. Nevertheless, should such departures be presumptively invalid? Just the opposite should be the case, but unfortunately public forum analysis often leads judges to improperly bind school officials to continue present practices, however flawed.

The standards of reasonableness and fairness proposed earlier for the articulation requirement would serve the court well in this case. The court is properly concerned with the inadequacy of the criteria employed, along with the inconsistent application of the school's policy. There was, unfortunately, no written regulation pertaining to the yearbook quotations, and the criteria of taste and appropriateness were porous, as the court correctly stated.

The inadequacy of the criteria applied by the school officials illustrates the wisdom of written policies. Ms. Stanton would have been better served by a regulation that gave notice based upon a "reasonable student" standard. Fairness would have been served by a consistent, evenhanded application of the policy. Ms. Stanton was treated unfairly, and she understandably expressed an all-too-frequent refrain: "What about them?" Given the character and content of previous quotations in the yearbook, and the absence of a written school policy that adequately notified a "reasonable student," the state's action, in this instance, seems unduly arbitrary.

One anticipated consequence of restricting the censorial authority of school officials may be that they will increasingly employ broad, content-based restrictions that close entire avenues to student expression. Here, absent broad discretionary authority, administrators may simply do away with any quotations rather than subject themselves to further litigation. This would hardly advance the free speech of students.

Conversely, when the courts limit the censorial authority of school officials, they may provide a haven for educators who do not want to censor student expression. Requiring officials to associate the school with student speech may help them to withstand censorial pressures from parents. Both scenarios are plausible, thereby illustrating the difficulty in predicting the consequences of judicial edicts regarding associative speech.

Granting school officials broad censorial authority over associative student speech may mistakenly justify any censorial action when even a modicum of funding, access, or supervision is involved. This is no small risk, given the strong impulse administrators have to avoid controversy. Indeed, permitting state officials to censor speech merely because they provide financial support for the speakers raises serious First Amendment problems.[72] Nonetheless, I believe that the proposed standards of fairness and reasonableness, pertaining especially to the articulation requirement, will temper such invidious actions. Of course, these standards are offered as a better approach than other alternatives, such as public forum analysis. It is, however, an imperfect approach, with significant risks and pitfalls.

Conclusion

Most of the litigation addressed in this chapter involves editorial control over school-sponsored student publications. Newspapers outside the public school environment are subjected to an array of controls involving their content and viewpoints. Direct control may be exercised, for example, by a newspaper's editorial board, its publisher, or even its staff. In addition, indirect censorial pressure may be brought to bear by advertisers and readers. In short, adult journalists rarely enjoy a free reign to have their articles published without restraint.

Nonetheless, the First Amendment is concerned with state censorship, and this creates an inevitable tension with regard to school-sponsored student publications. To declare that educators must not exercise any editorial control makes little sense, and poor constitutional law. Even Justice Brennan acknowledges that school officials may exercise editorial control over school-sponsored student publications if they serve legitimate educational interests, such as grammar and accuracy:

> [A] school may in its capacity as publisher of a school news-
> paper or producer of a school play "disassociate itself," . . .
> not only from speech that would "substantially interfere with
> [its] work . . . or impinge upon the rights of other stu-
> dents," . . . but also from speech that is, for example, ungram-
> matical, poorly written, inadequately researched, biased or
> prejudiced, vulgar or profane, or unsuitable for immature au-
> diences. A school must be able to set high standards for the
> student speech that is disseminated under its auspices —
> standards that may be higher than those demanded by some
> newspaper publishers or theatrical producers in the "real"
> world — and may refuse to disseminate student speech that
> does not meet those standards.[73]

Justice Brennan is correct in his argument. He does not go far
enough, however, for the inculcative function is a legitimate state
interest that is, on occasion, furthered by viewpoint discrimination.
If editorial control over school-sponsored publications is denied to
officials, who wields it? Surely, only a tortured argument could distinguish why the First Amendment permits the faculty adviser more
control than a school administrator. Such a stance can rest on principles of academic freedom for adult teachers, but becomes unconvincing when it rests on the First Amendment rights of students.
Leaving important editorial decisions to the student journalists,
even to the student editor, may be a wise pedagogical strategy, but it
is not one mandated by the First Amendment. The nature of student
journalism requires that tough decisions be made. Ultimately, the
responsibility should fall on school officials with substantial discretionary authority regarding the student speech with which they wish
to "associate."

Seven

Access to Information and Ideas

[Some] authorized person or body has to
make a determination as to what the library
collection will be. It is predictable that no
matter what choice of books may be made by
whatever segment of academe, some other
person or group may well dissent. The

ensuing shouts of book burning, witch

hunting and violation of academic freedom

hardly elevate this intramural strife to first

amendment constitutional proportions. If it

did, there would be a constant intrusion of

the judiciary into the internal affairs of the

school. Academic freedom is scarcely

fostered by the intrusion of three or even nine

federal jurists making curriculum or library

choices for the community of scholars.

Presidents Council, District 25 v. Community School Board

While toleration and association disputes involve direct student expression, indoctrination disputes consider whether the First Amendment confers upon public school pupils a "right to receive" information and ideas from third parties. The bulk of disputes over such a right concern the removal of books from school libraries.[1]

Island Trees v. Pico

The United States Supreme Court, in a 1982 plurality ruling, recognized a First Amendment "right to receive" for public school students. This case, entailing seven opinions, merits extensive discussion, for it reflects the precarious nature and character of the right.

In September 1975 a local school board justified the removal of the following books as "anti-American, anti-Christian, anti-Semitic, and just plain filthy":

> *Slaughterhouse-Five,* by Kurt Vonnegut, Jr.
> *The Naked Ape,* by Desmond Morris
> *Down These Mean Streets,* by Piri Thomas
> *Best Short Stories of Negro Writers,* ed. by Langston
>   Hughes
> *Go Ask Alice,* anonymous
> *A Hero Ain't Nothin' but a Sandwich,* by Alice Chil-
>   dress
> *Soul on Ice,* by Eldridge Cleaver
> *A Reader for Writers,* ed. by Jerome Archer
> *The Fixer,* by Bernard Malamud.

The members of the board concluded that it was their duty and ethical obligation to protect students from moral danger as surely as from physical and medical dangers.[2] Accordingly, the board ordered school officials to remove the books from school libraries and from the curriculum.[3]

Upholding the board's action, and stating that federal courts should not intervene in the daily operations of school systems, the district court granted administrators broad discretionary authority regarding educational policy.[4] It concluded that removing the books did not constitute "viewpoint discrimination," proscribed by the First Amendment. While questioning the wisdom of the board's actions, the court concluded that they did not constitute a sharp and direct infringement of any First Amendment right.[5]

The Second Circuit Court of Appeals reversed, with a three-judge panel issuing three separate opinions.[6] Delivering the opinion for the court, Judge Sifton found the board's criteria to be impermissibly broad and vague.[7] A concurring Judge Newman found the actions to constitute impermissible viewpoint discrimination.[8] A dissenting

Judge Mansfield saw the actions as reasonable and constitutionally permissible.[9]

In a plurality opinion authored by Justice Brennan, the United States Supreme Court affirmed.[10] The key question addressed: Does the First Amendment impose limitations upon the authority of a local school board to remove books from high school and junior high school libraries? The plurality noted that the issues raised were distinct from textbook, curricular issues in which school officials presumptively enjoy broad discretionary authority.[11] Furthermore, Justice Brennan stressed the special characteristics of a school library. For example, he noted that they embody "voluntary inquiry" as opposed to the mandatory character of classroom instruction. Thus, the plurality concluded that the inculcative function does not justify granting broad discretionary authority to school officials who seek to remove books from library shelves.[12]

The Court sharply distinguished between the removal of a book from the library and its initial acquisition. Removing books directly and sharply implicated the constitutional rights of students, for the First Amendment not only serves to foster individual self-expression but also to afford public access to discussion, debate, and the dissemination of information and ideas.[13]

While acknowledging the importance of the inculcative function, the Court nonetheless declared that the First Amendment limits the discretionary authority of school officials. More precisely, the plurality stated that the First Amendment entails a corollary right to receive ideas and information. This right to receive prepares students to participate in our pluralistic, often contentious society.[14]

Regarding school libraries, officials may not exercise their discretionary authority in a narrowly partisan or political manner.[15] The *Pico* plurality flatly stated that the Constitution does not permit the official suppression of ideas.[16] However, since educators must select the ideas and information students are exposed to during the school day, their motives for removing books become paramount. In other words, because discretionary decisions are necessary, the grounds for them may warrant judicial scrutiny. Thus, for the plurality the key factor in discerning impermissible viewpoint discrimination was the motivation behind the school board's actions.[17] Based upon the statements by the board members explaining what they felt to be their moral obligation, along with the presence of irregular removal procedures, the Court concluded that the board's motives were improper and thereby constituted impermissible viewpoint discrimination.[18] The Court acknowledged, however, that removal of library books was permissible if they were "pervasively vulgar" or if school officials reasonably questioned their "educational suitability."[19]

Justice Harry Blackmun, while concurring with the judgment, made a significant departure from the plurality's assertion of a student's First Amendment right to receive information and ideas. While the other four justices focused on the failure to provide information, he emphasized the state's decision to single out an idea for disapproval and then deny access to it.[20] He also rejected the plurality's assertion that such a right was somehow associated with the peculiar nature of the school library. Blackmun argued that if schools may be used to inculcate ideas, surely libraries may play a role in that process.[21]

Furthermore, Blackmun expressed doubt regarding a theoretical distinction between removing a book and failing to acquire a book. However, he noted a "profound practical and evidentiary distinction," since removal, more than failure to acquire, is likely to suggest that an impermissibly political motivation may be present. The justice argued that there are many legitimate reasons for not acquiring a book, but few legitimate reasons for removing one.[22]

For Blackmun, the primary challenge for the Court was reconciling the First Amendment with the inculcative function:[23]

> Concededly, a tension exists between the properly inculcative purposes of public education and any limitation on the school board's absolute discretion to choose academic materials. But that tension demonstrates only that the problem here is a difficult one, not that the problem should be resolved by choosing one principle over another.[24]

Accordingly, Blackmun drew upon *Tinker,* arguing that the school board must show that its action was not merely a ruse to avoid controversy or based on an "undifferentiated fear." Thus, Justice Blackmun concluded that the courts should strike down any "purposeful suppression of ideas."[25]

In dissent, Chief Justice Burger reformulated the issues into two related questions: Who runs our schools? Are values of morality, good taste, and relevance valid reasons for removing books? In sharp contrast to the plurality opinion, Burger argued that a school board ought not be required by the First Amendment to aid the speaker. He rejected the implication that if a writer has something to say the government must become a "slavish courier of the material of third parties."[26] Rather, school officials warrant substantial discretionary authority in this area in order to carry out their inculcative function. Not surprisingly, Burger concluded that such decisions ought to be made by local school authorities, not by federal judges.[27]

The chief justice characterized the plurality exception of "educational suitability" as a standardless phrase, since fulfilling the inculcative function demands that school boards make content-based decisions about the appropriateness of retaining materials in the school library and curriculum.[28] Finally, Burger declared that the government, here, did not "contract the spectrum of available knowledge"; instead, it merely chose not to be the conduit of particular information.[29]

A dissenting Justice William Rehnquist argued that public educators invariably make numerous decisions based on their own personal or moral values.[30] For him, the "right to receive" and the inculcative function are irreconcilable. He adamantly rejected a constitutional right of students to receive information.[31] For support, he noted that *Tinker* did not mention any such right, since it addressed solely the freedom to express.[32] For Rehnquist, the idea that students have a right of access, while on school grounds, to information other than that thought by their educators to be necessary goes against the very nature of inculcative schooling.

Education consists of the selective presentation and explanation of ideas. The effective acquisition of knowledge depends
upon an orderly exposure to relevant information. . . . Of necessity, elementary and secondary educators must separate the
relevant from the irrelevant, the appropriate from the inappropriate. Determining what information not to present to the
students is often as important as identifying relevant material.
This winnowing process necessarily leaves much information
to be discovered by students at another time or in another
place, and is fundamentally inconsistent with any constitutionally required eclecticism in public education.[33]

Justice Rehnquist attacked other elements of the plurality opinion
as well. If students enjoy a First Amendment "right to receive,"
"motive" should not matter, since both good and bad motives suppress ideas.[34] Similarly, Rehnquist failed to see why removal warrants greater judicial scrutiny than acquisition.[35] Finally, the "suppression of ideas" alleged by the plurality did not entail complete
denial of access, for the books were readily available elsewhere.[36]
For Rehnquist, then, denial of access in this context failed to cast a
"pall of orthodoxy" over the classroom. He concluded that the in-
consistencies and illogic of the limitations placed by Justice Brennan
on such a right illustrate that the right itself is misplaced in the
elementary and secondary school setting.[37]

A dissenting Justice Lewis Powell found the ruling to intrude
unduly into the daily operation of the public school system. He
offered high praise for the democratic character of school boards,
and he warned that such decisions invariably corrode boards' authority and effectiveness in carrying out their important duties.[38]

Powell cautioned that the ruling leads the judiciary down a slip-
pery slope, for it is difficult to limit, on a principled basis, a First
Amendment "right to receive" for public school students. Such a
right, for Powell, may well lead to student oversight of the purchase
of textbooks, the development of course curriculums, and teacher

employment, all of which would be unwise educational policy and poor First Amendment law.[39]

Right to Receive: Emergence and Rationale

On numerous occasions since the 1940s the Court has conferred a right to receive for adults. In a 1943 ruling, *Martin v. City of Struthers,* the Court acknowledged a right to receive home delivery of religious literature.[40] More than twenty years later, in *Stanley v. Georgia,* the Court declared an individual right to receive information and ideas in the privacy of one's home, including obscene materials.[41] That same year the Court, in *Red Lion Broadcasting Co. v. FCC,* found a public right of access to social, political, aesthetic, moral, and other ideas.[42] In 1974, the Court extended the right to include a prisoner's right to receive uncensored mail.[43] Two years later, in *Virginia State Board of Pharmacy v. Virginia Citizens Council,* the Court struck down a state statute that prohibited drug-price advertisements on the grounds that it violated the right of consumers to receive such information.[44] Significantly, before *Pico,* the Court refused to extend a right to receive to children, or to recognize its existence beyond the schoolhouse gate.

In *Pico,* the Court's rationale for extending a right to receive to public school students rests upon several claims and assertions that merit examination. The Court announced that removing books from school library shelves directly and sharply implicated the First Amendment rights of students because of the dual role of the amendment. One aspect fosters individual self-expression, while the other affords public access to debates, discussion, and the dissemination of information and laws.[45] Thus, in a marketplace of ideas, the right to receive opinions and information follows "ineluctably" from the sender's right to send them.[46]

The Court also argued that such a right is an essential predicate to the recipient's meaningful exercise of First Amendment freedoms.[47] When extended to students, this right to receive prepares them for active and effective participation in our pluralistic, often contentious society. In sum, the right to receive information protects students from school officials who wish to impose a "pall of orthodoxy."[48]

The rationale for extending a First Amendment right to receive to public school students also finds expression in lower court rulings. Here, the courts typically voice concern that school officials, with unfettered authority, will indirectly impose a "pall of orthodoxy" within the nation's public schools. In a ruling cited by the *Pico* plurality, a federal district court explains the importance of extending a right to receive to public school students:

> The library is "a mighty resource in the marketplace of ideas." . . . There a student can literally explore the unknown, and discover areas of interest and thought not covered by the prescribed curriculum. The student who discovers the magic of the library is on the way to a life-long experience of self-education and enrichment. That student learns that a library is a place to test or expand upon ideas presented to him, in or out of the classroom. The most effective antidote to the poison of mindless orthodoxy is ready access to a broad sweep of ideas and philosophies. There is no danger in such exposure. The danger is in mind control.[49]

Given the actions of school officials, such fears have some foundation. The following is a sampling of the books that educators have banned or have attempted to ban:

> *1984,* by George Orwell
> *Brave New World,* by Aldous Huxley
> *The Catcher in the Rye,* by J. D. Salinger
> *Of Mice and Men,* by John Steinbeck
> *The Merchant of Venice,* by William Shakespeare
> *The Adventures of Tom Sawyer,* by Mark Twain
> *The Adventures of Huckleberry Finn,* by Mark Twain
> *The Sun Also Rises,* by Ernest Hemingway

> *Black Like Me,* by John H. Griffin
> *Citizen Tom Paine,* by Howard Fast.[50]

The plurality in *Pico* understood that a "right to receive" for students should not be coextensive with that for adults, due to the special nature of both adolescents and the public schools. Therefore, the justices made a number of distinctions that substantially narrowed the scope of this right. Unfortunately, as the following section explains, this modification fatally undermines the Court's claim that the First Amendment confers a right to receive on public school students.

Pico Reconsidered

The First Amendment right of students to receive information and ideas established in *Pico* entails two related but arguable assertions. One distinguishes the character of the school library from the nature of the school curriculum. The plurality stated that a school library, no less than any other public library, is a place dedicated to quiet, to knowledge, and to beauty.[51] The Court also viewed the school library as the principal locus of students' freedom to inquire, to study and evaluate, and to gain new maturity and understanding.[52]

To buttress the claim of a unique role for school libraries, the plurality stressed the voluntary nature of the libraries. Students' selection of books is "entirely a matter of free choice," and school libraries afford them an opportunity for self-education and individual enrichment that is wholly optional.[53] Accordingly, the Court concluded that while the inculcative function may justify granting school officials absolute discretion in matters of curriculum, their authority becomes less expansive when extended "beyond the compulsory environment of the classroom, into the school library and the regime of voluntary inquiry that there holds sway."[54]

Despite the asserted special character of school libraries, the right to receive applies only to the removal of library books, not to their initial acquisition. The *Pico* Court recognized that local school boards have a substantial role to play in the initial selection of library materials, but it limited their authority to remove books.[55] Unfortunately, the Court fails to explain this distinction adequately. Instead, the Court suggests that the removal of library books presumptively infers that school officials are impermissibly suppressing ideas. Thus, for the plurality, the removal of library books demands greater judicial scrutiny than does their acquisition.

Regarding the special role of the school library, the plurality's claim is unconvincing. Even Justice Blackmun, in his concurring opinion, correctly rejected this assertion, noting that the school library also serves the inculcative function.[56] Admittedly, distinguishing the role of the school library from classroom instruction makes pedagogical sense. Such a distinction understands the voluntary nature of using library resources. However, it does not necessarily follow that because something makes sense it needs constitutional sanction. What makes up sound educational policy is not identical to wise First Amendment doctrine.

Similarly, by characterizing the high school curriculum as "compulsory" the *Pico* Court overstated the distinction between the reading of library books and classroom texts. Much of the curriculum is "elective," for rarely are all students required to take specific courses with similar reading assignments. For example, most pupils in high school, while required to fulfill a certain number of English credits, nonetheless may select from an array of classes, ranging from Greek mythology to American short stories. Furthermore, the library often plays an integral role in classroom assignments. This complementary curricular function suggests that the distinction between decisions about the school library and those about the curriculum is not as sharp or as decisive as the plurality argues.

The *Pico* Court also failed to explain adequately why the optional nature of library books entitles school officials to exercise less discretion than they possess regarding the curriculum. If the Court fears heavy-handed educators indoctrinating pupils, perhaps it should limit their discretionary authority over curricular decisions, rather than forbidding them to remove books from library shelves.[57]

The plurality's distinction between removal and acquisition is even less credible than the claim regarding the "unique nature" of the school library. Chief Justice Burger noted a fatal flaw in the plurality's reasoning:

> [If] the First Amendment commands that certain books cannot be removed, does it not equally require that the same books be acquired? . . . According to the plurality, the evil to be avoided is the "official suppression of ideas." . . . It does not follow that the decision to remove a book is less "official suppression" than the decision not to acquire a book desired by someone. Similarly, a decision to eliminate certain material from the curriculum, history for example, would carry an equal — probably greater — prospect of "official oppression."[58]

A dissenting Justice Rehnquist agreed, noting that the failure of a library to acquire a book denies access to its contents just as effectively as does the removal of a book.[59]

This distinction between acquisition and removal in effect allows library books to acquire "tenure." Once a book is placed on the library shelf, it is difficult to remove. A lower federal court explains why "book tenure" does not warrant First Amendment sanction:

> This concept of a book acquiring tenure by shelving is indeed novel and unsupportable under any theory of constitutional law we can discover. It would seem clear to us that books which become obsolete or irrelevant or where improperly selected initially, for whatever reason, can be removed by the same authority which was empowered to make the selection in the first place.[60]

Justice Blackmun provided a more persuasive rationale for distinguishing between removing a library book and acquiring it than did Justice Brennan. Although Blackmun questioned a theoretical dis-

tinction between removal and acquisition, he recognized a practical
and evidentiary difference between the two actions:

> [Removal], more than failure to acquire, is likely to suggest
> that an impermissible political motivation may be present.
> There are many reasons why a book is not acquired, the most
> obvious being limited resources, but there are few legitimate
> reasons why a book, once acquired, should be removed from a
> library not filled to capacity.[61]

Blackmun's argument fails to persuade, for there are more legitimate
reasons to remove a book from the library shelves than he implies. It
may be outdated, or inaccurate; it may be culled because of height-
ened awareness and concern over racism and sexism; perhaps a
newly appointed librarian wishes to revamp the collection according
to his or her own professional judgment. Together, legitimate reasons for removing library books exist beyond the space limitations
Blackmun mentions.

The *Pico* plurality's rationale for a student's right to receive information entails confusing, amorphous standards and principles. According to this decision, the right to receive prohibits impermissible
"suppression of ideas."[62] However, recognizing that public education invariably excludes certain ideas and information, the plurality
confined the suppression principle to the removal of books from
school libraries. The intent or purpose underlying officials' actions
will determine whether the removal violates the First Amendment.[63]
Thus, when public school authorities restrict access to ideas with
which they disagree, they are imposing a "pall of orthodoxy" that is
not permitted by the First Amendment.[64]

Focusing on the intentions and motives of the school officials
leads the courts into a treacherous thicket in which judges must
discern official motives. The relevance of motive and purpose may
also be questioned, since, as Justice Rehnquist argued, bad and good
motives alike deny access to the books removed.[65] If students truly

enjoy a constitutional right to receive information, it is difficult to see why motive and purpose of suppression determine First Amendment protection.[66]

The examples used by the plurality to illustrate the suppression principle underscore the hollowness of this "standardless standard":

> [School officials] rightly possess significant discretion to determine the content of their school libraries. But that discretion may not be exercised in a narrowly partisan or political manner. If a Democratic school board, motivated by party affiliation, ordered the removal of all books written by or in favor of Republicans, few would doubt that the order violated the constitutional rights of the students. . . . The same conclusion would surely apply if an all-white school board, motivated by racial animus, decided to remove all books authored by blacks or advocating racial equality and integration. Our Constitution does not permit the official suppression of ideas.[67]

While such actions may well violate the First Amendment, these scenarios are not analogous either to *Pico* or to other cases brought before the courts.[68] Thus, the suppression principle helps resolve hypothetical disputes, rather than the types of actions typically brought before the courts.[69]

Removing school library books does not necessarily constitute suppressing ideas. In *Pico*, Justice Rehnquist correctly argued that for denial of access to be synonymous with suppression of ideas the denial must be relatively complete. Such is not the case in school library disputes, for the ideas and information are typically available in other accessible locations.[70] For example, in *Pico* the banned books were displayed at the local public library after being removed from the school library, thereby making them accessible to any inquisitive student.[71]

The suppression principle becomes even more questionable in light of the legitimate reasons for library book removals conceded by the principle's proponents. For example, the *Pico* plurality noted that removing a book would be permissible if school officials demonstrated that it was "pervasively vulgar."[72] Such an exception, however, sanctions highly subjective determinations by school officials, since "vulgarity," like obscenity, may lie in the eye of the beholder.[73] Similarly, the plurality failed to explain why vulgarity must be "pervasive" in order to be permissible. As Chief Justice Burger argued, vulgarity may reside in one poem, or a particular page, and still overshadow the rest of the book.[74] The following passage from one of the books banned by the *Pico* school officials, *Soul on Ice,* by Eldridge Cleaver, makes the point:

> There are white men who will pay you to fuck their wives. They approach you and say, "How would you like to fuck a white woman?" "What is this?" you ask. "On the up-and-up," he assures you. "It's all right. She's my wife. She needs black rod, is all. She has to have it. It's like a medicine or drug to her. She has to have it. I'll pay you. It's all on the level, no trick involved. Interested?"[75]

The *Pico* plurality suggests that such a passage, on its own, does not provide sufficient grounds to remove a book from a library.

Similarly, the *Pico* plurality permits removing books because of "educational suitability,"[76] although the Court failed to explain what the words mean. This standard undoubtedly pertains to library books that lie beyond the academic and intellectual capabilities of students. It would also likely include books that are inaccurate or outdated in information and ideas, such as almanacs and historical works. But certainly a reasonable interpretation of "educational suitability" would incorporate the inculcative function. Here, books could be educationally unsuitable due to the values they express, be they racial, sexual, religious, or political. Thus, school officials could plausibly use this broad standard to justify the removal of almost any book from the school library. Chief Justice Burger agrees:

"Educational suitability," however, is a standardless phrase. This conclusion will undoubtedly be drawn in many—if not most—instances because of the decisionmaker's content-based judgment that the ideas contained in the book or the idea expressed from the author's method of communication are inappropriate for teenage pupils.[77]

Justice Blackmun's exceptions to the suppression principle fare no better than do the plurality's "pervasive vulgarity" and "educational suitability" standards. Blackmun conceded that along with "space" or "financial" considerations, educators may control the content of the school library by withholding a book from students on the following grounds:

> First Amendment principles would allow a school board to refuse to make a book available to students because it contains offensive language . . . , or because it is psychologically or intellectually inappropriate for the age group, or even, perhaps, because the ideas it advances are "manifestly inimical to the public welfare." . . . And, of course, school officials may choose one book over another because they believe that one subject is more important, or is more deserving of emphasis.[78]

Given such an array of legitimate reasons for book removals—offensiveness, appropriateness, public welfare—any school official with a modicum of imagination and acumen could forge a defense that would likely satisfy such loose criteria.

Focused Balancing: Unnecessary and Inappropriate

The problematic distinctions made by the *Pico* plurality, and the porous standards and principles applied in the case, reflect the precarious assertion that public school students enjoy a First Amendment right to receive information and ideas. Such a right incorrectly presumes that public school libraries are, in principle and in fact, "marketplaces of ideas." Public schools are state institutions that, by their very nature, restrict the flow of communication. Yet, the plurality in *Pico* declared that the state must not "contract the spectrum of available knowledge."[79] Such a view cannot be reconciled with the decisions that confront our public educators every day. Chief Justice Burger, in his *Pico* dissent, explains:

> In the very course of administering the many-faceted operations of a school district, the mere decision to purchase some books will necessarily preclude the possibility of purchasing others. The decision to teach a particular subject may preclude the possibility of teaching another subject. A decision to replace a teacher because of ineffectiveness may by implication be seen as a disparagement of the subject matter taught.[80]

Given that school authorities, be they administrators or teachers, invariably control the content of ideas and information presented in school, a right to receive unduly restricts their discretionary authority. Disputes over removing books from public school libraries involve educational policy rather than First Amendment doctrine. In sum, such actions should be about whether school officials should remove the books, not whether they have the authority to do so.

A student's right to receive information fails to recognize that the First Amendment rights of young people are not coextensive with those of adults. The precedents relied upon by Justice Brennan in the plurality decision carve out a limited right for adults, but they do not extend such a right to children. Nor do they apply directly to the public school context.[81] As argued in Chapter Two, the constitutional rights of students in general should not be coextensive with those of adults, for children require autonomy from adult authority even as they require adult protection. Thus, students need to experience some degree of free speech if they are to develop into independent, responsible adults. However, adults may legitimately restrict this freedom, since young people are often too immature and vulnerable to make critical decisions. Such restrictions are especially appropriate when determining what third party expression students will be exposed to during the school day.

Proponents of a right to receive confuse educational policy making and constitutional law. However unsettling and discomforting we may find the removal of library books — and there are good reasons for outrage — we must keep in mind that what we believe school officials ought to do is often distinct from what the Constitution requires of them.[82]

Two lower court rulings illustrate this critical distinction between educational policy making and First Amendment doctrine.[83] A poem, "The City to a Young Girl," appeared in an anthology of writings by adolescents, *Male and Female under Eighteen.*[84] This poem referred to "horney lip-smacking men" begging for "pussy," "tit," "ass," and "cunt."

In 1977, this poem spurred the school board of Chelsea, Massachusetts, to order the anthology's removal from the public high school library. Subsequently, a suit was brought before the federal district court, seeking an order requiring that the anthology be returned to the library intact.[85] The parties to the suit from the high school included students, the librarian, the chairwoman of the English department, and an English teacher; they were joined by the Right to Read Defense Committee, which was formed at the time of the school board action. The suit charged the board with violating the First Amendment rights of the students, faculty, and library staff. The board argued that it merely exercised its legitimate statutory authority to oversee the curriculum of the school.

Although it had been on the library shelves for more than a year, the anthology first came to the attention of the school board when a parent, troubled by the poem, complained directly to the board chairman. While the school board never claimed the poem to be unconstitutionally obscene, the chairman found it to be "offensive" and "filthy," and he sought its removal without reading any other part of the anthology. He promptly called an emergency board meeting to discuss the matter and wrote an article for the local daily paper expressing his outrage.

The school superintendent, however, reviewed the entire anthology and concluded that, as a whole, the book had educational value except for the poem in question and one other word in one other poem.[86] Predictably, interested parties participated in several board meetings, which were characterized by an array of proposals, amendments, and recommendations.[87] After the board's final decision to remove the anthology, the plaintiffs sought relief from the federal judiciary.

The school board claimed unconstrained authority to take books off library shelves, arguing that since it was not required to purchase a book it had a free reign to remove it.[88] The federal district court acknowledged a broader power regarding selection than for removal. However, the district court noted that the reason for the removal was the board's conclusion that the theme and language of the poem was "offensive." The purpose or motive for the ban was important to the court, given that reasons underlying the actions of school officials may determine their constitutionality.[89] The court, guided by the *Tinker* decision, believed that removal of library books requires local officials to demonstrate some substantial and legitimate government interest.[90] The interest need not be classroom order and discipline, but it must be of comparable importance. The court found no such interest, and it pointedly noted that parental sensitivities are not the full measure of what is proper education.[91]

The district court's reasoning is unconvincing on a number of grounds. For one, it framed the issues too narrowly, focusing only upon a dubious "right to read":

> There is more at issue here than the poem City. If this work may be removed by a committee hostile to its language and theme, then the precedent is set for removal of any other work.

> The prospect of successive school committees "sanitizing" the
> school library of views divergent from their own is alarming,
> whether they do it book by book or one page at a time. . . .
> What is at stake here is the right to read and be exposed to
> controversial thoughts and language — a valuable right subject
> to First Amendment protection.[92]

More is at stake, however, than a student's right to receive; as Chief
Justice Burger correctly noted in *Pico,* these disputes represent a
struggle over who runs our public schools. Here, the parties bringing
suit include not only students but also high school faculty and the
school librarian. Understood in this light, the dispute is among educators competing for authority over the content of library materials, rather than being merely a dispute between a tyrannical school
board and inquisitive students. Removing the anthology from the
library thus becomes a matter of educational policy rather than constitutional law.

   Along with the issue of who runs the schools, this case, like *Pico,*
considers whether the values of morality, good taste, and relevance
to education are valid reasons for school board decisions concerning
the contents of a school library.[93] While the board chairman regarded the poem as "filthy," note the federal court's characterization
of it:

> City is not a polite poem. Its language is tough, but not obscene.
> Whether or not scholarly, the poem is challenging and thought-
> provoking. It employs vivid street language, legitimately offen-
> sive to some, but certainly not to everyone. The author is writ-
> ing about her perception of city life in rough but relevant
> language that gives credibility to the development of a sensitive
> theme. ["City's"] words may shock, but they communicate.[94]

Whose judgment and sensitivities ought to prevail? Such determinations, by and large, should be made by school officials rather
than federal judges. A federal court should not interpret the First

Amendment in a way that requires school officials to make this poem available to students. Certainly, the school board's decision may be unwise educational policy, but it should not be construed as an infringement upon the First Amendment rights of public school students. Such rulings confuse what educators ought to do with what the Constitution requires of them.

Whose judgment about the appropriateness of the poem ought to prevail? That of the school board? The high school librarian? Parents? A federal judge? In its decision (see p. 137 in this volume), the court misconstrues the nature of the school library. Although sound educational policy might permit the anthology to remain on the library shelf, the federal court erred in declaring that the First Amendment prohibits the school board from removing the book. The court looked to *Tinker* for guidance, yet the facts of the case, and the issues raised, were profoundly distinct. In *Right to Read,* we find no direct punishment of students, nor do we witness any viewpoint discrimination regarding political or social ideas. Instead, we find a school board deciding to remove one book from the library. This remains a far cry from an intolerant school board that directly punished students engaged in passive, symbolic, nondisruptive political expression.

While most cases regarding a "right to receive" involve removing library books, it should not be surprising that it infiltrates into curriculum decisions as well. The following case underscores why a coherent rationale for this right remains elusive.

For several years a school district in Minnesota included in its secondary curriculum a film version of Shirley Jackson's short story "The Lottery," in which the citizens of a small town randomly select one person to be stoned to death each year. In addition, students viewed a "trailer" film aimed at stimulating discussion and analysis of the story. During the 1977–78 school year, a group of parents and other citizens sought to have the films removed from the district's curriculum. Their objections focused on the alleged violence in the movies and their purported impact on the religious and family values of students.

At an informational meeting with disgruntled parents, a group of teachers defended the films' place in the curriculum. Unswayed, a group of parents formally requested that the school board remove the films. A review committee appointed by the board recommended that the films not be used at the junior high school level, but that they remain in the high school curriculum, so long as parents could prohibit their children from attending screenings. Still dissatisfied, the parents appealed the committee's recommendations to the board; by a four to three vote, the members chose to eliminate the films from the district's curriculum. At this meeting, the school board gave no reasons for its decision.

In *Pratt v. Independent School District No. 831, Forest Lake*, three students brought suit to have the films reinstated, arguing that their First Amendment rights had been violated in a case of viewpoint discrimination. The federal district court ruled in their favor and ordered the films returned to the curriculum.

The school board argued that the films placed an exaggerated and undue emphasis on graphic violence and bloodshed, making them neither appropriate nor suitable for showing in a high school classroom.[95] The district court felt that this argument failed to constitute cognizable, credible evidence as to any legitimate reason for excluding the films from the curriculum.[96]

The Eighth Circuit Court of Appeals affirmed, declaring that school officials may not impose a "pall of orthodoxy" on "classroom instruction which implicates the state in the propagation of a particular religious or ideological viewpoint."[97] Accordingly, the court held that the students had a right to be free from official conduct that was intended to suppress the ideas expressed in the films.[98]

Expressing much skepticism about the board's judgment and motives, the circuit court found the views of the films put forth by the high school faculty and professional educators more convincing:

> Opponents of "The Lottery" focused primarily on the purported religious and ideological impact of the films. They contended that the movies must be removed from the curriculum

because they posed a threat to the students' religious beliefs and family values.

In contrast to these value-laden objections, several teachers testified that "The Lottery" is an important American short story, that the film was faithfully adapted from the short story, that the story stimulates students to consider new ideas, and that the films are an effective teaching tool and involve students who might not otherwise read the story. Moreover, an empirical study conducted by two University of Maryland education professors was provided to the board, which concluded that the film version of "The Lottery" produced no negative effects on students in terms of violence and attitudes toward family or religious values. Forest Lake teachers attending the February and March meetings concurred with this assessment of the effect of the films.[99]

Accordingly, the circuit court imposed a substantial burden of proof upon the school board, requiring a showing of a substantial and reasonable governmental interest for interfering with the students' right to receive information.[100] Unfortunately for the board, the court found that its claim of excessive violence in the films was not supported by the evidence and that it merely constituted an after-the-fact cloak for censorship. Similarly, although the school board had allowed Jackson's short story to remain available to teachers and students in the library, the court nonetheless held that this fact was not decisive.

The symbolic effect of removing the films from the curriculum is more significant than the resulting limitation of access to the story. . . . "The Lottery" is not a comforting film. But there is more at issue here than the sensibilities of those viewing the films. What is at stake is the right to receive information and to be exposed to controversial ideas — a fundamental First Amendment right. If these films can be banned by those opposed to their ideological theme, then a precedent is set for the removal of any such work.[101]

By calling forth the specter of pervasive censorship, the Eighth Circuit Court of Appeals erred in several ways. Again, the issues involved concern educational policy rather than First Amendment doctrine. Even though the faculty was not a party in the suit, it is clear that several teachers opposed the board's decision to ban the movies. The larger issue is not whether students have a First Amendment right to view the films, but whether teachers, school administrators, or elected board members have final say regarding the content of school curriculum.

The court too readily dismissed the board's decision, denigrating the grounds for it as "value-laden objections." The court failed to explain adequately why the taste, values, morality, and sensitivities of the school board are not legitimate grounds for excluding the films from the curriculum.

The Court also implied that because the parents' objections to the movie version of "The Lottery" included religious objections, the school board must not respond to their concerns. Certainly, the court should be alert to undue religious pressure upon educational policies. But should religious objections by parents make school board decisions presumptively invalid, merely because the board and certain parents agree that a film is "inappropriate"?

Finally, we should be wary of federal court decisions that mandate the content of school curriculums to this degree. The banning of the films did not constitute "suppression of ideas," for the short story was readily available in the school library. Furthermore, unlike *Pico,* this case concerned the curriculum, not the removal of a library book.

Conclusion

A First Amendment right to receive information and ideas should not be extended to public school students. In general, their constitutional rights need not be coextensive with those of adults. While this point is generally conceded by the proponents of such a right, their effort to forge a modified right to receive cannot be defended on either theoretical or practical grounds. Public schools, including their libraries, are not amenable to "marketplace of ideas" claims, for such arguments confuse preferred educational policy decisions with sound First Amendment doctrine.

In this context, the inculcative function cannot be sufficiently reconciled with a right to receive, and therefore efforts at balancing, however "focused," are doomed to failure.[102] Focused balancing, then, holds little utility for resolving disputes over a right to receive, for it presumes an accommodation may be made between the stated government interests and the First Amendment. Indeed, employing this approach to decide disputes involving the right to receive would present the courts with formidable difficulties. Because the distinction between the selection and removal of library books is unconvincing (as is that between the content of library books and curriculum texts), the courts would have to scrutinize a major portion of the decisions made by public educators. Such a course would severely test both the capacity and legitimacy of the courts.

Removing books from a library rarely implicates the First Amendment interests of students, and therefore no judicial "balancing" is necessary, except in truly exceptional circumstances. Educators ought to enjoy substantial discretion in determining the content of the school library, a discretion that is identical for both acquisition and removal. Perhaps the most insightful opinion found in *Pico* was also the briefest. Justice Sandra Day O'Connor provides a succinct, convincing summation of the argument presented in this chapter:

> If the school board can set the curriculum, select teachers, and determine initially what books to purchase for the school library, it surely can decide which books to discontinue or remove from the school library so long as it does not also interfere with the right of students to read the material and to discuss it. . . . I do not personally agree with the Board's action

with respect to some of the books in question here, but it is not the function of the courts to make the decisions that have been properly relegated to the elected members of school boards. It is the school board that must determine educational suitability, and it has done so in this case.[103]

Eight

A Matter of Degree

A society is not an undifferentiated heap of
individuals, equal, at the same level of
"authority" and "right." It is a continuing
entity, continuously regenerating itself,
always pregnant, always with a generation
in limbo, always with a part of itself in a

condition of tutelage. The distinction

between minor and adult—however much

we may be baffled by borderline problems,

by demands for adequate criteria, by

administrative difficulties—is fundamental

and inescapable. There is no society which

does not recognize the distinction or mark,

by some rite of passage, the movement from

one condition to the other—the achievement,

as we would say, of the age of consent. No

single set of principles can adequately

govern both minor and adult; we need both

caterpillar principles and butterfly principles.

Joseph Tussman, *Government and the Mind*

Given the dual pursuits of academic excellence and classroom order, educational reform efforts invariably affect the constitutional rights of public school students. Accordingly, the United States Supreme Court has granted them some measure of First Amendment speech protection. Not surprisingly, the Court's effort displeases both those who oppose extending any constitutional protection to student speech and those who support expansive First Amendment protection for young people.

In determining what, if any, First Amendment rights students ought to enjoy, it must be recognized that the aims of free speech and public education are both congruent and oppositional. Furthermore, the inculcative function should be the decisive factor when courts balance the legitimate state interests entailed in public schooling with the aims and values of the First Amendment. According to these premises, public school students should enjoy the following First Amendment protections.

First, engaging in direct, independent, nondisruptive speech should receive considerable protection under the Constitution. Those engaged in symbolic speech, in writing for underground newspapers, or in expressing themselves away from school premises are presumptively protected from punitive and censorial actions taken by educators.

Second, however, student expression that requires the assistance of school authorities should receive less protection under the First Amendment. Officials should enjoy greater discretion in restricting or censoring student speech that entails funding, supervision, or the use of school facilities. Although such authority should be substantial, it should not be unlimited.

Finally, public school students should not enjoy a First Amendment right to receive information — educators warrant substantial authority to determine the content of school materials and curriculums. Thus, disputes involving classroom texts or library resources should not be construed as conflicts over the independent First Amendment rights of students.

These parameters, taken together, suggest an intermediate level of First Amendment protection for student expression. It recognizes pupils as constitutional persons, acknowledges the legitimate inculcative mission of public educators, and appreciates the distinction between sound constitutional doctrine and desirable educational policy.

Legitimacy and Capacity

> The question of when and how much the Supreme Court
> should intervene to overturn acts of the democratically elected
> political branches is, needless to say, a difficult one, and there
> has been no shortage of commentary on the subject. In fact,
> the country has pondered the question of judicial activism
> versus judicial restraint for a long time, and the controversy
> has intensified in the wake of the modern Court's long and
> continuing record of activism. After two centuries of debate,
> we appear hardly closer to an answer today than we were in
> 1789.[1]

A thoughtful discussion of student free speech should address the
legitimacy and capacity of the courts to resolve First Amendment
disputes.[2] "Legitimacy" pertains to the kinds of cases the courts
ought to hear; "capacity" refers to the courts' ability to resolve the
issues and cases brought before them. As Donald Horowitz points
out, the two are related, for a court wholly without capacity undermines its legitimacy, and a court that lacks legitimacy suffers from
diminished capacity.[3]

Legitimacy typically involves the authority of courts to displace
the value choices of elected legislative officials by judicially fash-
ioned policies.[4] For some, judicial legitimacy requires that courts ad-
here to certain procedural attributes, typically embodied in a limited
judicial role. Here, courts are considered intrinsically different from
other political institutions, and adherence to "courtness" is especially necessary because the courts are otherwise not accountable to
the political order.[5] Conversely, others link judicial legitimacy to
results and outcomes rather than to an orthodox judicial process.
Thus, accountability rests on courts' ability to do justice and otherwise contribute to bettering the human condition. In this view, what
courts contribute to attaining society's goals is more important than
preserving a fictional — or at best theoretical — autonomy.[6]

For resolving disputes over public education, Michael Rebell and

Arthur Block argue that judicial competency entails five related elements: the court must articulate a workable principle or standard to guide future actions by interested parties; hear from all of the interested parties; receive and assimilate the relevant evidence; resolve evidentiary conflicts; and develop and implement a workable remedy.[7]

With regard to the First Amendment rights of public school students, we should presume courts have both the legitimacy and the capacity to hear and resolve such disputes. Surely, safeguarding First Amendment rights and scrutinizing state censorship are legitimate exercises of judicial authority.[8]

Judicial competency should be presumed, since the courts have established a long-standing, substantial body of First Amendment law that, for the most part, satisfies the criteria set forth by Rebell and Block. Similarly, First Amendment disputes over student speech do not entail acutely contentious aspects of judicial authority, such as custodial supervision of schools, prisons, or hospitals. Despite the claims of Justice Hugo Black and others who reject conferring any independent First Amendment rights on students, we are not concerned with justices creating a fundamental right from "whole cloth." Likewise, controversial affirmative decrees in which the courts "command" rather than "constrain" are rarely at issue, with the possible exception of the misguided "right to receive" cases. Nonetheless, while the legitimacy and capacity of the courts to resolve such disputes should be presumed, judicial scrutiny regarding the authority of school officials to censor student expression poses difficulties for the courts. Justice Brennan explains:

> Public education serves vital national interests in preparing the Nation's youth for life in our increasingly complex society and for the duties of citizenship in our democratic Republic. . . . The public educator's task is weighty and delicate indeed. It demands particularized and supremely subjective choices among diverse curricula, moral values, and political stances to teach or inculcate in students, and among various methodolo-

> gies for doing so. Accordingly, we have traditionally reserved
> the "daily operation of school systems" to the States and their
> local school boards. . . . We have not, however, hesitated to
> intervene where their decisions run afoul of the Constitution.[9]

Therefore, declaring that the courts have the institutional legitimacy
and capacity to resolve student speech disputes merely provides a
starting place for the defense of my argument. Other compelling and
troublesome concerns and objections to that argument and analysis
merit more extensive discussion.

Responding to Criticisms

The First Amendment protection for public school students proposed here is strikingly similar to that established by the Supreme
Court over the past two decades. Like the Court, I argue that students' free speech rights ought not be coextensive with those of
adults. While I applaud the merits of *Tinker,* the Court's subsequent
departure from it — evident in *Fraser* and *Hazelwood* — correctly
recognizes the importance of the inculcative function and the distinct character of toleration and association disputes. This argument, however, differs significantly from the status quo, rejecting
both the public forum analysis employed in *Hazelwood* and the
"right to receive" erected by the *Pico* plurality. Nonetheless, the criticisms directed toward the current state of students' First Amendment rights are, by and large, relevant to this argument, and they
demand attention.

Unwarranted First Amendment Protection

Some jurists and commentators oppose even a modicum of First
Amendment protection for public school students. Justice Black, in
his *Tinker* dissent, suggested that school officials ought to enjoy

unfettered authority to restrict student speech.[10] He argued that children should not be considered "constitutional persons," for they require control, discipline, and supervision, rather than greater independence and autonomy. For Black, granting students independent First Amendment rights merely fueled a destructive attitude of permissiveness toward our nation's youth.[11] He solemnly warned that uncontrolled and uncontrollable liberty is an enemy to domestic peace.[12]

Similarly, David Diamond argues that the Court should apply a minimal rationality test in judging whether school authorities have violated the First Amendment.[13] In advocating unfettered authority for educators, these critics fail to understand that, in certain contexts, official restriction of student speech implicates the First Amendment. Although school officials ought to be granted substantial discretionary authority to fulfill their important inculcative duties, students merit some constitutional protection.

Insufficient First Amendment Protection

Perhaps the more troublesome criticisms of my argument are those advocating greater First Amendment protection for students than I recommend.

The "marketplace of ideas" metaphor holds a prominent place in free-speech discussions, and defenders of greater First Amendment rights for students often apply it to public schools. The majority in *Tinker* embraced this view:

> The vigilant protection of constitutional freedoms is nowhere more vital than in the community of American schools. . . .
> The classroom is peculiarly the "marketplace of ideas." The Nation's future depends upon leaders trained through wide exposure to that robust exchange of ideas which discovers truth "out of a multitude of tongues, [rather] than through any kind of authoritative selection."[14]

For Tyll van Geel, the First Amendment requires school officials to expose students to a wide range of viewpoints, thereby transforming public schools into academic marketplaces via a "principle of fairness." This principle involves a quite demanding judicial standard, for van Geel argues that when a school provides instruction on moral or political matters it must adequately and objectively cover the issues directly and indirectly touched upon by the materials.[15] In addition, the coverage must be "fair," meaning that it accurately and objectively reflects opposing views on the issues and that reasonable attention is devoted to these positions.[16]

In advocating such noble standards van Geel fails to understand that public schools are not, in practice or in principle, marketplaces of ideas. Indeed, in certain respects they may be viewed as the antithesis of academic marketplaces. Public schools are state institutions that inevitably exercise at least a modicum of authoritarian paternalism and unsupervisable discretion.[17] Public educators invariably inculcate values, for they dispose students to accept some opinions and values over others.[18] Malcom Stewart elaborates:

> [To] a large extent the state will and should be perceived as giving its endorsement to the materials presented through its educational programs. By endorsement I mean something significantly different from agreement . . . proper education can take place only if students make such an inference. Part of the educator's function is to give students a sense of both the range and limits of ongoing public debate: students must be shown that there exists a middle ground between blind adherence to a monolithic orthodoxy and the nihilistic belief that no idea is better than any other.[19]

Schools are not marketplaces in which an unlimited number of ideas may compete for the attention of pupils. Nor are students informed, voluntary "consumers" exercising autonomy in selecting information and ideas that they deem to be essential to their education. The monopolic position of the state in selecting course materials, regulating student conduct, and inculcating values undermines any reasonable understanding of what constitutes a "marketplace." By applying the dominant metaphor for adult free speech to student expression, we misconstrue the aims and practice of our nation's public schools.

Understating the Risks and Dangers

Some critics will certainly charge that my argument misstates the risks and dangers of the inculcative function. They point out that students are quite vulnerable to indoctrination. The state is, in large part, the sole speaker to the student audience and the sole determiner of the content of school materials; furthermore, through compulsory education laws, students are made a captive audience.[20] This monopolic position of the government, these commentators declare, elevates its standing and prestige, helps to establish the perception that its beliefs and propositions as true, and thereby gives students the impression of government infallibility. This, in turn, allows government to predominate over alternative voices with fewer resources.[21] Together, proponents of greater First Amendment protection characterize the inculcative function as excessively coercive, oppressive, and strangling, making it the identical twin of state indoctrination, which is presumptively forbidden by the First Amendment.

Other commentators, however, take a more modest position, noting that while a tension exists between the Constitution and the inculcative function, a balance, however approximate, remains within our grasp. For them, my argument strikes no such balance, since it does not give sufficient weight to the First Amendment. Robert Gordon, for example, offers a less crude view of inculcation, asserting that its legitimacy depends upon the values transmitted, and the means employed, by school officials in fulfilling it. Gordon distinguishes two inculcative approaches available to school officials. One is prescriptive, or directive, and involves transmitting information and accepted truths to passive and absorbent students.[22]

This approach typically involves coercion, exhortation, and systems of reward and punishment, and is functionally no different from indoctrination.

The other approach is discursive, or analytical, and is characterized by active inquiry by both student and teacher. Here, instructors present values for discussion and analysis, thereby emphasizing reason and dialogue.[23] Gordon argues that the First Amendment substantially restricts the values school officials may inculcate and that school authorities should be limited to espousing those beliefs necessary to maintain a democratic system of government.[24] In his view, legitimate values are those explicitly or implicitly found in the Constitution. The explicit values include justice, liberty, national defense, domestic tranquillity, and the promotion of the general welfare. The implicit values include privacy, due process, majority rule, individual autonomy, equality before the law, and the sanctity of private property.[25] While educators may employ the prescriptive approach for inculcating constitutional values, Gordon argues that nonconstitutional values must be inculcated via the discursive approach.

Concerns over indoctrination are certainly reasonable, given the questionable censorship imposed by school officials, but such fears should not fatally undermine the legitimate inculcative function. Again, public education, by its nature, limits the range of ideas and information presented to students within the school's curriculum, and public educators must invariably make conscious choices on the basis of content.[26] Therefore, the risks and dangers of inculcation are ultimately unavoidable. Furthermore, critics overstate the risks of the process by ignoring the numerous checks on the inculcative power of public educators besides the First Amendment. The influence of friends, family, religious groups, and the mass media all operate, at times, to counterbalance the inculcative function. In addition, millions of children attend private schools, and public education remains highly decentralized, thus making indoctrination sporadic at best.[27]

Gordon's effort to temper the ills of inculcation remains quite suspect, for his enumerated list of explicit and implicit constitutional values could arguably validate any action by school officials to restrict student expression. A cursory examination of constitutional law reveals profound disagreement over the meaning of "justice," "privacy," "equality," and "due process." The porous nature of these values, combined with his curious assertion that the First Amendment mandates particular pedagogical strategies, illustrate the futility of severing the inculcative function from public education. While the Socratic method may be better suited for transmitting nonconstitutional values than a more rigid approach, it is difficult to see how the First Amendment requires teachers to employ it in the classroom.

The inculcative function may, in some contexts, be synonymous with coercive indoctrination. Mark Yudof's assessment of government speech illustrates the problematic character of public education.

> The paradoxical nature of government speech makes it difficult to decide which way constitutional protection should cut. Expression by government is critical to democratic processes, but the power of governments to communicate is also the power to destroy the underpinnings of government by consent. The power to teach, inform, and lead is also the power to indoctrinate, distort judgment, and perpetuate the current regime. Persuasion, like coercion, can be employed for many different purposes, some more acceptable than others.[28]

Legitimate concerns over the inculcative function certainly ought to be acknowledged and addressed. However, supporters of widespread access to ideas and information must understand that the First Amendment should not be the only, or even the primary, bulwark against public educators who wish to indoctrinate pupils in a harmful, coercive fashion. Student speech disputes entail important educational policy decisions, and nonjudicial arenas provide ample opportunities for free-speech advocates to triumph. They may prevail by pressuring legislators, participating in school board elections, employing academic freedom, and galvanizing parental and public support. Child advocates and First Amendment watchdogs must recognize that lawsuits are but one approach — and not necessarily the proper or most effective means — to secure free speech for public school students.[29]

Unwarranted Trust in Authorities

Given the disturbing record of school boards in flagrantly violating the Constitution with regard to matters of equal protection, freedom of religion, and unreasonable searches and seizures, some critics may attack my argument for placing too much trust in local school officials. These critics understandably and correctly note the censoring of literary works by Twain, Hemingway, Steinbeck, and Vonnegut, among others. Accordingly, they often portray school officials, particularly administrators and board members, as people all too eager to act foolishly and unlawfully in trampling on the constitutional rights of students. Thus, public school officials do not merit the judicial deference sanctioned in my argument.

In addition to questioning the judgment of locally elected school officials, some commentators wonder about the extent to which they represent democratic ideals and principles. Robert Keiter, for example, questions the representativeness of many school boards and whether their policies reflect community values and views.[30] He notes that school board contests are characterized by low voter turnouts, with greater numbers of affluent citizens more likely to participate. Most board elections are nonpartisan and uncontested, with incumbents overwhelmingly being returned to office. Keiter points out that citizens generally have little knowledge about public education and the local school system.[31] Finally, he measures school governance against classic democratic theory, and finds the boards' performance lacking.[32]

While the censorial efforts of local school boards often deserve our disapproval, the courts should presume them to be legitimate political bodies. Keiter's assessment of school board contests may well be valid, but they are not decisive, for they arguably apply to most popular elections held in this country. Congressional races, for example, are marked by low voter turnout, an ill-informed electorate, virtually unbeatable incumbents, and participation skewed toward affluent constituencies. Therefore, Keiter fails to explain why school officials merit less trust than other representatives. Another commentator, Malcom Stewart, argues that the presumption of public approval in the school context is greater than that for other elected decision makers. While this point may be challenged, Stewart correctly argues that the basic principle of democratic theory is that decisions made by popularly elected officials have the presumptive approval of the community.[33] This presumption, of course, does not end the discussion over judicial intervention, for the First Amendment limits the extent to which majorities can use the ballot to accomplish their will.[34] Nonetheless, Stewart correctly argues that when a school board fails to reflect community sentiment accurately, then disgruntled citizens should become more actively involved in formulating educational policy.[35] Stewart concludes that if government content discrimination is always suspect, then the notion of the public educator is a contradiction in terms, since her or his job is inherently a process of continual discrimination of this sort.[36]

How much trust should be granted to local school officials is, of course, a matter of degree. What burden of proof should the courts impose on school censors? To answer this question, we must recognize that the government has a variety of roles. Justice Rehnquist, in his *Pico* dissent, linked the authority to regulate speech to the various functions of government. He argued that the government may act in capacities other than as a sovereign issuing coercive commands; when it acts as an employer, property owner, or educator, the First Amendment "may speak with a different voice."[37] Rehnquist believes that First Amendment jurisprudence would be bet-

ter served by candidly recognizing that state educators are subject to less stringent limitations than are sovereign agents of the
state, including such other elected bodies as town councils and state
legislatures.[38]

The special characteristics of public schooling reflect the paradoxical nature of state authority. Certainly, much about such schooling is coercive. But to see only this aspect of the educational enterprise results in unwarranted distrust of locally elected school
officials. Joseph Tussman explains:

> The tendency, when we think of government, to think simply
> of coercion, of commands and sanctions, of law-maker, judge
> and police, is simply a failure of understanding and imagina-
> tion. Consider, for example, the public school. It is a govern-
> mental institution as clearly as is the fire department, the
> board of public health, the municipal court. The governing
> structure of a state university is as much a part of government
> as is the city council of the community in which the university
> is located. The schoolteacher works for the government as un-
> mistakably as does the deliverer of the daily mail. In fact, if we
> consider the question afresh, we may well conclude that the
> public-school teacher in America today is the most appropri-
> ate symbol of government in action, the paradigmatic govern-
> ment agent. Government acts in a variety of modes and it is
> not precluded, simply by virtue of a narrow misconception of
> government as essentially coercive, from acting deliberately
> and appropriately on the mind. There is, of course, a coercive
> aspect of government, and there is something to be said for the
> view that government ought to enjoy, if not monopoly, at least
> coercive supremacy. But to say this is not to say that the es-
> sence of government is coercion or that it can only act in this
> mode. A parent may also lay down rules, warn, and punish,
> but that does not define the essence of parenthood or the limits
> of the parental role.[39]

The Promotion of Indoctrination

Still other commentators maintain that the First Amendment and the inculcative function cannot be readily reconciled or "balanced," and that my argument fails in this respect because it undervalues the First Amendment interests implicated in student speech disputes. They conclude that the First Amendment should presumptively supersede the inculcative function whenever conflicts arise. For example, van Geel believes that a student's "freedom of belief" ought to be coextensive with that of an adult citizen, thereby calling for a remarkably stringent standard of judicial scrutiny.[40] For him, if governmental policies directed toward the indoctrination of youth are to survive constitutional challenge, they must serve a vital governmental end by closely tailored means. Thus, actions by school officials would be impermissible if they were found to be counterproductive or otherwise ineffective in reaching the proffered goal.[41] Similarly, the state must rest its actions on factual findings and prove that less restrictive means are not available to achieve its vital interest.[42]

In addition, van Geel argues that a stringent standard of judicial review is necessary to secure democratic principles and ideals. This, in turn, requires the government to be neutral about values and viewpoints. In following this approach, the courts advance the democratic and constitutional ideals of individual autonomy. Thus, van Geel argues that students warrant a constitutional "right of autonomy" entailing a "freedom of belief" that includes both religious and nonreligious views. He wants the courts to establish a "principle of fairness" to protect students from the inculcation of political ideas, attitudes, viewpoints, ideologies, values, or beliefs.[43] For him, the First Amendment presupposes that opinions, viewpoints, and beliefs expressed by citizens — including students — are not the products of deliberate governmental efforts to shape and condition those beliefs.[44] Otherwise, the First Amendment could serve no meaningful function in a democratic society, and the right of free speech would become irrelevant.[45]

Van Geel's right to autonomy implies the following: belief is to be formed, if at all, through dialogue; students must be exposed to controversy and encouraged to think critically about values; schools must prepare students to resist manipulation and lead them to identify themselves as human beings first and citizens second; and the inculcative function is inconsistent with a student's right to autonomy.[46] Van Geel also believes that, if educational institutions are not subject to the same constitutional constraints as other governmental agencies, students will not understand the values of a democratic, participatory society. They will, instead, become members of a passive, alienated citizenry disillusioned by an arbitrary government.[47]

As Bruce Hafen explains, those calling for a stringent standard of judicial scrutiny confuse forging sound First Amendment doctrine with formulating educational policy.

> [The] precise way in which a given student's intellectual skill might best be developed is a crucial question of educational policy, more than it is a question of constitutional law. . . . It is the place of educational philosophy and methodology to find, according to each pupil's needs, the right balance between too much direction and not enough. By contrast, it is the place of constitutional interpretation to avoid actual harm at the utter extremes of that process.[48]

Van Geel's argument, and other calls for "state neutrality," ignore the fact that democratic principles and practices require that the government act rather than adopt a passively neutral role. Unfortunately, neutral arguments reflect romantic notions of a mythical intellectual autonomy. This myth suggests that each individual, operating on neutral principles, makes an independent selection in the marketplace of ideas.[49] However, people do not possess this ability to make choices at birth; they have to obtain the necessary skills, and therein lies a problem for those who question the legitimacy of the inculcative function. The illusion of intellectual autonomy implies that there is some analytical distinction between skills and ideology and, further, that we can train an individual to solve problems without instilling certain powerful preconceptions as to what the answers are likely to be.[50]

The inculcative function is crucial in establishing and maintaining a "moral community," which is a predicate for the self-governing, autonomous citizenry sought by First Amendment advocates like van Geel. The demand for school officials to remain neutral regarding the inculcation of values corresponds, consciously or unconsciously, to the tenets of cultural relativism. Here, a student must learn not only to understand and respect the moral perspective of another — a worthy goal in a pluralistic, liberal society — but must also somehow treat this viewpoint as being just as valid as her or his own.[51] Liam Grimley correctly points out the difficulties of this approach: "It is one thing to recognize that every individual has equal rights in the area of belief and value, but something quite different to say that every individual's values are equally valid and sound. To hold such a position is not only logically undesirable, it is logically impossible."[52]

Similarly, Andrew Oldenquist argues that while private institutions, such as churches and families, enjoy a right to engage in moral suasion, public institutions — especially public schools — have an obligation to do so, because they are essential instruments created by a society to perpetuate its existence. To argue that a society lacks the right to teach children basic morality is tantamount to suggesting that it has no right to exist.[53]

It is a mistake to view the transmission of culture as a diminution of our freedom, for it is the very condition of becoming a person. We are, to a significant degree, "social constructs," although there is dramatic disagreement over their contours and features. We cannot combat the evils of state indoctrination by denying the right of public educators to inculcate community values, however defined, for neither intellectual freedom nor free speech is a product of benign neglect.[54] If free speech is a fundamental element of democratic governance, as I believe it is, then surely government may legitimately transmit and encourage certain values, such as tolerance and re-

straint, that are necessary for free speech to operate. As Joseph Tussman wisely reminds us, the teaching power is the most fundamental
and alienable power of the state, for it is crucial to the nation's self-
preservation.[55]

Conclusion

Developing a democratic citizenry in this country, of course, requires
both appreciation for and exercise of freedom of expression, which
is guaranteed under the First Amendment. However, citizens of a
democracy must exhibit a "democratic character," which is a product of "deliberate nurture." Tussman explains:

> A community is constituted by — its very existence depends
> upon — a condition or state of mind. It is not a mere collection
> of physical entities or a herd of biological organisms. It is a
> continuing organization of persons related by shared under-
> standings, commitments, agreements, attitudes.
>
> There are, of course, reductionist tendencies at work as we
> attempt to understand the community or polity, and it is al-
> ways tempting to settle for something more tangible and more
> easily observable than a state of mind. Heads and hands can be
> counted, the movements of herds can be mapped, the play of
> power traced and measured. But we can never, in these terms,
> tell the central human story — the story of conscious human
> beings creating and nurturing common enterprises and fellow-
> ships in pursuit of shared visions, struggling for some sem-
> blance of peace, freedom, justice, dignity, brotherhood. To try
> to understand a community without attempting to grasp the
> condition of mind that distinctively constitutes it is to system-
> atically miss the point. Not simply because a community is the
> sort of entity that happens, also, to "have" a mind: but, more
> fundamentally, because community is a condition of mind. If
> the constitutive condition of mind is lost or absent, there sim-

ply is no community in any significant sense. . . . The democratic way of life is not a condition men fall into if only the
mind is left to its own devices; it is not the fruit of spiritual an-
archy or neglect. However much democracy may differ from
other forms of polity it is not, in principle or in practice, an exception to the rule that the community may legitimately act,
through government, on the mind. The burdens and responsibilities are merely greater.[56]

Constructing the moral community necessary for sustaining a
self-governing, pluralistic society is a formidable task. Children
must learn to think critically about authority, as well as to confer
obedience, if they are to develop into democratic citizens.[57] Public
educators are expected to prepare and train children for entry into
the adult community—which requires extensive guidance and control—without sacrificing students' capacity to act as autonomous,
self-governing citizens. These dual expectations require balancing.
To speak in absolutes of children's liberation or unfettered authority
ignores the complexities of granting public school students constitutional protection.[58]

Since the socialization of children is inevitable, the pressing questions are who will do the socializing and what information and
values will be inculcated.[59] To repeat, it is simply not possible (nor
is it desirable) for public educators to convey only information, for
the very manner of its selection and presentation will lead to the
transmission of certain values and beliefs.[60] The First Amendment
should curb the excesses of the inculcative function. But it should
not unduly infringe upon its legitimate and essential role in public
education.

Notes

Chapter One

1. *Tinker v. Des Moines Independent Community School District*, 393 U.S. 503, 505 (Supreme Court of the United States, 1969).

2. *Tate v. Board of Ed. of Jonesboro, Ark., Spec. Sch. Dist.*, 453 F.2d 975, 978 (Circuit Court of Appeals, Eighth Circuit, 1972).

3. *Klein v. Smith*, 635 F.Supp. 1440, 1441 (District Court of Maine, 1986).

4. For a sample of this debate, see Harvey Holtz et al., *Education and the American Dream: Conservatives, Liberals, and Radicals Debate the Future of Education* (Granby, Mass.: Bergin and Garvey, 1989).

5. National Commission on Excellence in Education, *A Nation at Risk: The Imperative for Educational Reform* (Washington, D.C.: Government Printing Office, 1983); reprinted in Beatrice Gross and Ronald Gross, eds., *The Great School Debate: Which Way for American Education?* (New York: Simon and Schuster, 1985), pp. 23–49.

6. Concern over a crisis in public schooling continues into the 1990s. See, for example, Mary Jordan, "On Track Toward Two-Tier Schools," *Washington Post National Weekly Edition* 10, no. 3 (May 31–June 6, 1993): pp. 31–32.

For an alternative analysis suggesting that public schools do not warrant such harsh critiques, see Peter Schrag, "The Great School Sell-Off," *American Prospect* (Winter 1993): pp. 34–43 ("Given the enormous changes in the demographics of American schools and considering the idiot culture in which our students live most of the day, it's surprising the schools have done as well as they have" [p. 38]).

7. For a sample of reports on and critiques of American education, see Mortimer Jerome Adler, *The Paideia Proposal* (New York: Macmillan, 1982); Ernest L. Boyer, *High School: A Report on Secondary Education in America* (New York: Harper and Row, 1983); Business–Higher Education Forum, *America's Competitive Challenge: The Need for a National Response* (Washington, D.C., 1983); College Entrance Examination Board, *Academic Preparation for College: What Students Need to Know and Be Able to Do* (New York, 1983); John I. Goodlad, *A Place Called School: Prospects for the Future* (Highstown, N.J.: McGraw-Hill, 1983); J. Lynn Griesemer and Cornelius Butler, *Education under Study: An Analysis of Recent Major Reports on Education* (Chelmsford, Mass.: Northeast Regional Exchange, 1984); National Commission on Excellence in Education, *A Nation at Risk;* and National School Public Relations Association, *Excellence: Your Guide to Action Now* (Arlington, Va., 1984).

8. See, for example, Northeast Regional Exchange, "The National Reports on Education: A Comparative Analysis," in Gross and Gross, *The Great School Debate,* pp. 50–71.

9. National Commission on Excellence in Education, *A Nation at Risk,* pp. 23–49.

10. Ibid., pp. 26–36.

11. Ibid., p. 24.

12. Ibid., p. 27.

13. Edward B. Fiske, "The Report That Shook Up Schools," *Washington Post National Weekly Edition* 10, no. 26 (May 3–9, 1993): p. 28.

14. Of course, these reports received severe condemnation as well as praise. See, for example, Henry A. Giroux and Peter McLaren, "Teacher Education and the Politics of Engagement: The Case for Democratic Schooling," *Harvard Educational Review* 56, no. 3 (August 1986): pp. 213–38. (They argue that such criticisms of public schools measure their utility against its contribution to economic growth and cultural uniformity. "Similarly, at the heart of the present ideological shift is an attempt to reformulate the purpose of public education around a set of interests and social relations that define academic success almost exclusively in terms of the accumulation of capital and the logic of the marketplace" [p. 218].)

15. William K. Muir, "Teachers' Regulation of the Classroom," David L. Kirp and Donald N. Jensen, eds., *School Days, Rule Days* (Philadelphia: Falmer Press, 1986), p. 110.

16. Oliver C. Moles, "Trends in Student Misconduct: The Seventies and

Eighties" (paper presented at the annual meeting of the American Educational Research Association, Washington, D.C., April 20–24, 1987), p. 2. ERIC ED 286954.

In this examination of the First Amendment rights of public school students, I define school discipline to be the formal system involving school rules, who breaks them, and what punishment occurs. Therefore, I consider how students may express themselves without fear of official punishment, as well as the rules and regulations school officials may employ in restricting student expression. For an overview of the literature regarding discipline and order, see Elizabeth Lueder Karnes, Donald D. Block, and John Downs, *Discipline in Our Schools: An Annotated Bibliography* (Westport, Conn.: Greenwood Press, 1983).

17. See, for example, Edmund T. Emmer, *Classroom Management for Secondary Teachers*, 2d ed. (Englewood Cliffs, N.J.: Prentice-Hall, 1989).

18. David A. Sabatino et al., *Discipline and Behavioral Management* (Rockville, Md.: Aspen Systems, 1983), pp. 29–84.

19. Robert W. Jones, "Coercive Behavior Control in the Schools: Reconciling 'Individually Appropriate' Education with Damaging Changes in Educational Status," *Stanford Law Review* 29 (1976): pp. 93–125.

20. Muir, "Teachers' Regulation of the Classroom," p. 110.

21. See, for example, Mary Jordan, "I Will Not Fire Guns in School," *Washington Post National Weekly Edition* 10, 36 (July 5–11, 1993): p. 31 ("As the 1993 school year ends, the final tally of weapons found in Los Angeles public schools is expected to top the 765 found last year").

22. Robert J. Rubel, *The Unruly School* (Lexington, Mass.: Lexington Books, 1977), p. 133.

23. Rodger W. Bybee and E. Gordon Gee, *Violence, Values, and Justice in the Schools* (Boston: Allyn and Bacon, 1982), p. 4.

24. Ibid., p. 20.

25. See, for example, Joan McDermott, "Crime in the School and in the Community: Offenders, Victims, and Fearful Youths," *Crime and Delinquency* 29, no. 2 (1983): pp. 270–82; see also Moles, "Trends in Student Misconduct." ERIC ED 286942.

26. Alec M. Gallup, *The Eighteenth Annual Gallup Poll of the Public's Attitudes toward the Public Schools* (Bloomington, Ind.: Phi Delta Kappa Research Foundation, 1986). ERIC ED 283928.

27. Edwin Meese III, Charles W. Hartman Memorial Lecture (delivered at the University of Mississippi, March 19, 1987). ERIC ED 279943, p. 12.

28. William J. Bennett, *What Works: School without Drugs* (Washington, D.C.: United States Department of Education, 1987), p. vii.

29. Bybee and Gee, *Violence, Values, and Justice,* p. 2.

30. *New Jersey v. T.L.O.,* 105 S.Ct. 733, 747 (Supreme Court of the United States, 1985) (Powell, J.: concurring).

31. Ellen Jane Hollingsworth, Henry S. Lufler, and William H. Clune, *School Discipline: Order and Autonomy* (New York: Praeger, 1984), p. 18.

32. Ibid., p. 19.

33. See, for example, Mary Metz, *Classrooms and Corridors* (Berkeley and Los Angeles: University of California Press, 1978), p. 243.

34. Muir, "Teachers' Regulation of the Classroom."

35. See, for example, Richard M. Merelman, "Democratic Politics and the Culture of American Education," *American Political Science Review* 74 (1980): p. 319. (Merelman argues that order is an organizational, not an educational, imperative [p. 324]).

36. David L. Kirp, "Proceduralism and Bureaucracy: Due Process in the School Setting," *Stanford Law Review* 28 (1976): p. 858. (The quotation cited is from Herbert A. Simon, *Administrative Behavior* [New York: Macmillan, 1957], p. 100.)

37. See, for example, Irwin A. Hyman and James H. Wise, eds., *Corporal Punishment in American Education* (Philadelphia: Temple University Press, 1979); see also: Esther P. Rothman, *Troubled Teachers* (New York: David McKay, 1977); and Stanley W. Rothstein, *The Power to Punish: A Social Inquiry into Coercion and Control in Urban Schools* (Lanham, Md.: University Press of America, 1984).

38. Carl F. Kaestle, "Social Change, Discipline, and the Common School in Early Nineteenth Century America," *Journal of Interdisciplinary History* 9 (1978): pp. 1–17.

39. Lawrence M. Friedman, "Limited Monarchy: The Rise and Fall of Student Rights," in Kirp and Jensen, eds., *School Days, Rule Days,* p. 241.

40. Sabatino et al., *Discipline and Behavioral Management,* p. 5.

41. See, for example, Hollingsworth, Lufler, and Clune, *School Discipline;* see also: Adah Maurer, *Paddles Away: A Psychological Study of Physical Punishment in Schools* (Palo Alto, Calif.: R and E Research Association, 1981); and Lee E. Teitelbaum, "School Discipline Procedures: Some Empirical Findings and Some Theoretical Questions," *Indiana Law Journal* 58, no. 4 (1983): pp. 547–96.

42. Sabatino et al., *Discipline and Behavioral Management,* p. 92.

43. Maurer, *Paddles Away,* p. 4.

44. Rothstein, *The Power to Punish,* p. 171.

45. Merelman, "Democratic Politics," p. 324.

46. Sabatino et al., *Discipline and Behavioral Management,* p. 111–61.

47. For a general discussion, see Henry S. Lufler, "Pupils," in Stephen

Thomas, ed., *The Yearbook of School Law: 1988* (Topeka, Kans.: National Organization on Legal Problems of Education [NOLPE], 1989). Regarding drug testing, see, for example, *Chicago Tribune,* September 17, 1989, p. 1. Regarding searches and seizures, see, for example, *Chicago Tribune,* September 17, 1989, p. 24; see also "A Threat to Freedom," *Time,* September 18, 1989, p. 28. Regarding "beepers," see, for example, *Wall Street Journal,* December 16, 1988, p. A10.

48. See, for example, *Tinker v. Des Moines Independent Community School District,* 393 U.S. 503 (Supreme Court of the United States, 1969); *Bethel School District No. 403 v. Fraser,* 106 S.Ct. 3159 (Supreme Court of the United States, 1986); and *Hazelwood School Dist. v. Kuhlmeier,* 108 S.Ct. 562 (Supreme Court of the United States, 1988).

49. See, for example, *New Jersey v. T.L.O.,* 105 S.Ct. 733 (Supreme Court of the United States, 1985), and *Cason v. Cook,* F.2d 188 (Circuit Court of Appeals, Eighth Circuit, 1987).

50. See, for example, *Ingraham v. Wright,* 430 U.S. 651 (Supreme Court of the United States, 1977).

51. See, for example, *Givens v. Poe,* 346 F.Supp. 202 (District Court of North Carolina, 1972), and *Goss v. Lopez,* 419 U.S. 565 (Supreme Court of the United States, 1975).

52. See, for example, "Wild in the Streets," *Newsweek,* August 2, 1993, pp. 40–46, and "Kids Growing Up Scared," *Newsweek,* January 10, 1994, pp. 42–49.

53. *Tinker v. Des Moines Independent Community School District,* 393 U.S. 503 (Supreme Court of the United States, 1969).

54. See, for example, Samuel Bowles and Herbert Gintis, *Schooling in Capitalist America* (New York: Basic Books, 1976); see also Joel Spring, *The Sorting Machine Revisited* (White Plains, N.Y.: Longman, 1989).

55. See, for example, Kirp and Jensen, *School Days, Rule Days;* see also Arthur E. Wise, *Legislated Learning* (Berkeley and Los Angeles: University of California Press, 1979).

56. See, for example, Beatrice Gross and Ronald Gross, eds., *The Children's Rights Movement* (Garden City, N.Y.: Anchor Press, 1977); see also: Patricia A. Vardin and Illene N. Brody, eds., *Children's Rights: Contemporary Perspectives* (New York: Teachers College Press, 1979); Laurence D. Houlgate, *The Child and the State: A Normative Theory of Juvenile Rights* (Baltimore, Md.: Johns Hopkins University Press, 1980); and Richard Farson, *Birthrights* (New York: Macmillan, 1974).

57. Leon Shaskolsky Sheleff, *Generations Apart* (New York: McGraw-Hill, 1981), p. 16.

58. See, for example, Mark N. Bonaguro, "*Hazelwood School District*

v. Kuhlmeier: How Useful Is Public Forum Analysis in Evaluating Restrictions on Student Expression in the Public Schools?" *John Marshall Law Review* 22, no. 2 (1988): pp. 403–19; see also: Elletta Sangrey Callahan, "*Hazelwood School District v. Kuhlmeier:* The Court Declines to Tinker with Students' Free Press Rights," *Journal of Contemporary Law* 15, no. 1 (1989): pp. 1–30; David A. Diamond, "The First Amendment and Public Schools: The Case against Judicial Intervention," *Texas Law Review* 59: p. 477; and Dinita L. James, "The School as Publisher: *Hazelwood School District v. Kuhlmeier,*" *North Carolina Law Review* 67, no. 2 (1989): pp. 503–16.

59. Walter A. Kamiat, "State Indoctrination and the Protection of Non-State Voices in the Schools: Justifying a Prohibition of School Library Censorship," *Stanford Law Review* 35, no. 2 (1983): pp. 497–535.

60. See, for example, Bruce C. Hafen, "Developing Student Expression through Institutional Authority: Public Schools as Mediating Structures," *Ohio State Law Journal* 48, no. 3 (1987): pp. 663–731.

Chapter Two

1. Franklin E. Zimring, *The Changing Legal World of Adolescence* (New York: Free Press, 1981), p. x.

2. Ibid., p. xi.

3. Larry J. Siegel and Joseph J. Senna, *Juvenile Delinquency: Theory, Practice, and Law* (St. Paul, Minn.: West, 1981), p. 305.

4. Robert H. Bremner, *Children and Youth in America: A Documentary History* (Cambridge, Mass.: Harvard University Press, 1971), vol. 1, p. 103.

5. Ibid.

6. Ibid.

7. Ibid., p. 38.

8. Ibid., pp. 108–28.

9. Ibid., p. 36.

10. Ibid., p. 103.

11. F. Raymond Marks, "Detours on the Road to Maturity: A View of the Legal Conception of Growing Up and Letting Go," *Law and Contemporary Problems* 39, no. 3 (1975): pp. 80–85.

12. Siegel and Senna, *Juvenile Delinquency,* p. 305.

13. Ibid., p. 85.

14. Marks, "Detours on the Road to Maturity," p. 78.

15. Ibid., p. 86.

16. Zimring, *Changing Legal World of Adolescence,* p. 32.

17. Ibid., pp. 32–40.

18. Ibid., p. 34. (Progressive child savers included Sara Cooper of the National Conference of Charities and Corrections, Lucy Flowers of the Chicago Women's Association, Sophia Minton of the New York Committee on Children, Judge Richard Tuthill, and the penologist Enoch Wines.)

19. Lee E. Teitelbaum, "The Psychological Rights of the Child and . . . The Law," in Stuart N. Hart, ed., *Viewpoints in Teaching and Learning 58,* no. 2 (1982): p. 118.

20. Christopher Lasch, *Haven in a Heartless World: The Family Besieged* (New York: Basic Books, 1977), p. 15.

21. Robert H. Bremner, *Children and Youth in America: A Documentary History* (Cambridge, Mass.: Harvard University Press, 1971), vol. 2, pp. 649–65.

22. Ibid., p. 1422.

23. Ibid.

24. Siegel and Senna, *Juvenile Delinquency,* p. 319.

25. Bremner, *Children and Youth in America,* vol. 1, p. 502–23.

26. Lasch, *Haven in a Heartless World,* p. 15.

27. Charles E. Silberman, *Criminal Violence, Criminal Justice* (New York: Random House, 1978), p. 310.

28. Ibid.

29. Ibid., p. 29. For a general discussion of this point, see Anthony M. Platt, *The Child Savers: The Invention of Delinquency* (Chicago: University of Chicago Press, 1969).

30. Lasch, *Haven in a Heartless World,* pp. 4–5.

31. For a general discussion, see Platt, *The Child Savers.*

32. Bremner, *Children and Youth in America,* vol. 1, p. 653.

33. Siegel and Senna, *Juvenile Delinquency,* pp. 310–11.

34. Ibid., p. 311.

35. Ibid., p. 659.

36. See, for example, Sanford J. Fox, "Juvenile Justice Reform: A Historical Perspective," *Stanford Law Review* 22 (1970): p. 1187; see also Platt, *The Child Savers.*

37. Silberman, *Criminal Violence, Criminal Justice,* p. 316.

38. Ibid., p. 314.

39. Ibid., pp. 311–12.

40. Ibid., p. 312.

41. Ibid.

42. *In re Gault,* 387 U.S. 1 (Supreme Court of the United States, 1967).

43. See, for example, Samuel M. Davis and Mortimer D. Schwartz, *Children's Rights and the Law* (Lexington, Mass.: Lexington Books, 1987); see also Zimring, *Changing Legal World of Adolescence.*

44. See, for example, David Gottlieb ed., *Children's Liberation* (Englewood Cliffs, N.J.: Prentice-Hall, 1973).

45. See, for example, Richard Farson, *Birthrights* (New York: Macmillan, 1974).

46. Diane Ravitch, *Revisionists Revised* (New York: Basic Books, 1978), p. 7.

47. Norman K. Denzin, "Children and Their Caretakers," in Gottlieb, *Children's Liberation,* pp. 125–43; see also George B. Leonard, "How School Stunts Your Child," in Gottlieb, *Children's Liberation,* pp. 145–66.

48. Denzin, "Children and Their Caretakers," pp. 127–36.

49. Leonard, "How School Stunts Your Child," p. 153.

50. Peter B. Meyer, "The Exploitation of the American Growing Class," in Gottlieb, *Children's Liberation,* p. 45.

51. Platt, *The Child Savers,* p. 176.

52. Ibid.

53. Not surprisingly, this revisionist critique of Progressive reformers has been challenged; see, for example, J. Lawrence Schultz, "The Cycle of Juvenile Court History," *Crime and Delinquency* (1973): pp. 457–76.

54. Farson, *Birthrights,* pp. 12–13.

55. See, for example, Ravitch, *Revisionists Revised.*

56. Ibid., p. 7.

57. Meyer, "Exploitation of the American Growing Class," p. 52.

58. See, for example, Marian Wright Edelman, *Families in Peril* (Cambridge, Mass.: Harvard University Press, 1987).

59. See, for example, Shirley Camper Soman, *Let's Stop Destroying Our Children* (New York: Hawthorn Books, 1974).

60. See, for example, Edelman, *Families in Peril.*

61. Zimring, *Changing Legal World of Adolescence,* p. 37.

62. See, for example, Lynn Sametz and Caven S. McLoughlin, eds., *Educators, Children, and the Law* (Springfield, Ill.: Charles C. Thomas, 1985); see also Jack C. Westman, *Child Advocacy* (New York: Free Press, 1979).

63. See, for example, Edelman, *Families in Peril.*

64. "Social Environment," from *Report to the President: White House Conference on Children* (Washington, D.C.: Government Printing Office, 1970), in Gottlieb, *Children's Liberation,* pp. 167–81.

65. See, for example, Edelman, *Families in Peril;* see also National Commission on Excellence in Education, *A Nation at Risk: The Imperative*

for Educational Reform (Washington, D.C.: Government Printing Office, 1983), reprinted in Beatrice Gross and Ronald Gross, eds., *The Great School Debate: Which Way for American Education?* (New York: Simon and Schuster, 1985), pp. 23–49.

66. Teitelbaum, "Psychological Rights of the Child," p. 114.

67. See, for example, Onora O'Neill, "Children's Rights and Children's Lives," *Ethics* (April 1988) (O'Neill argues that child advocates ought to focus upon adult obligations, rather than the rights of children [p. 462].)

68. Teitelbaum, "Psychological Rights of the Child," p. 118.

69. Ibid., p. 117.

70. Ibid.

71. Ibid., p. 116.

72. *Declaration of the Rights of the Child* (United Nations Resolution 1386) (New York, 1973).

73. Beatrice Gross and Ronald Gross, eds., *The Children's Rights Movement* (Garden City, N.Y.: Anchor Books, 1977).

74. Ibid.

75. Farson, *Birthrights*.

76. Ibid., p. 135.

77. Ibid., pp. 154–74.

78. See, for example, Gottlieb, *Children's Liberation*.

79. Teitelbaum, "Psychological Rights of the Child," p. 118.

80. Ibid., p. 119.

81. Ibid.

82. Ibid., p. 122.

83. Ibid.

84. Ibid., p. 120.

85. Ibid., p. 126.

86. Ibid.

87. Hillary Rodham, "Children's Rights: A Legal Perspective," in Patricia A. Vardin and Ilene N. Brody, eds., *Children's Rights: Contemporary Perspectives* (New York: Teachers College Press, 1979), p. 31.

88. *Prince v. Massachusetts,* 321 U.S. 158 (Supreme Court of the United States, 1944).

89. Ibid., p. 165.

90. Davis and Schwartz, *Children's Rights and the Law,* p. 54.

91. *Prince v. Massachusetts,* 321 U.S. 158, 168 (Supreme Court of the United States, 1944).

92. Davis and Schwartz, *Children's Rights and the Law,* p. 55.

93. *Ginsberg v. New York,* 390 U.S. 629 (Supreme Court of the United States, 1968).

94. Ibid., p. 640.

95. *New York v. Ferber,* 458 U.S. 747 (Supreme Court of the United States, 1982).

96. Ibid., p. 757.

97. Ibid.

98. Ibid., p. 759.

99. Ibid., p. 761.

100. Ibid., p. 763.

101. Ibid., p. 764.

102. *H.L. v. Matheson,* 450 U.S. 398 (Supreme Court of the United States, 1981).

103. A parental consent statute was struck down in *Planned Parenthood of Central Missouri v. Danforth,* 428 U.S. 52 (Supreme Court of the United States, 1976).

104. *H.L. v. Matheson,* 450 U.S. 398, 408 (Supreme Court of the United States, 1981).

105. See, for example, *Hodgson v. Minnesota,* 110 S.Ct. 2926 (Supreme Court of the United States, 1990); see also *Ohio v. Akron Center for Reproductive Health,* 110 S.Ct. 2972 (Supreme Court of the United States, 1990).

106. *Planned Parenthood v. Casey,* 112 S.Ct. 2791 (Supreme Court of the United States, 1992).

107. *Carey v. Population Services, Intern.,* 431 U.S. 678 (Supreme Court of the United States, 1977); see also *Michael M. v. Superior Court of Sonoma County,* 450 U.S. 464 (Supreme Court of the United States, 1981). (In a plurality opinion, the Court upheld California's statutory rape law, which applied only to female victims.)

108. *Bellotti v. Baird,* 443 U.S. 622 (Supreme Court of the United States, 1979).

109. Ibid., p. 633.

110. Ibid., pp. 638–39.

111. *Planned Parenthood v. Casey,* 112 S.Ct. 2791, 2835 (Supreme Court of the United States, 1992).

112. *In re Gault,* 387 U.S. 1 (Supreme Court of the United States, 1967).

113. Ibid., p. 13.

114. See, for example, Robert M. Horowitz and Howard A. Davidson, eds., *Legal Rights of Children* (Colorado Springs, Colo.: McGraw-Hill, 1984), pp. 4–5; see also Teitelbaum, "Psychological Rights of the Child," pp. 121–22.

115. Teitelbaum, "Psychological Rights of the Child," p. 121.

116. Ibid., pp. 121–22.

117. *In re Winship*, 397 U.S. 358 (Supreme Court of the United States, 1970).

118. Laurence H. Tribe, *American Constitutional Law*, 2d ed. (Mineola, N.Y.: Foundation Press, 1988), p. 741.

119. *In re Winship*, 397 U.S. 358 (Supreme Court of the United States, 1970).

120. *Gault* gets very compromised over time. For a detailed discussion, see Donald L. Horowitz, *The Courts and Social Policy* (Washington, D.C.: Brookings Institution, 1977).

121. *Parham v. J.R.*, 442 U.S. 584 (Supreme Court of the United States, 1979).

122. *Schall v. Martin*, 467 U.S. 253 (Supreme Court of the United States, 1984).

123. *Parham v. J.R.*, 442 U.S. 584, 602 (Supreme Court of the United States, 1979).

124. Davis and Schwartz, *Children's Rights and the Law*, p. 72.

125. Gary B. Melton, *Reforming the Law: Impact of Child Development Research* (New York: Guilford Press, 1987), pp. 238–39.

126. See, for example, Marian Wright Edelman, *The Measure of Our Success: A Letter to My Children and Yours* (New York: HarperCollins, 1992).

127. C. John Sommerville, *The Rise and Fall of Childhood* (Beverly Hills, Calif.: Russell Sage, 1982), p. 225.

128. Ibid., p. 208.

129. Radical critiques of public education pay little attention to securing constitutional rights for students. See, for example, Henry A. Giroux and Peter L. McLaren, eds., *Cultural Pedagogy, the State, and Cultural Struggle* (Albany: State University of New York Press, 1989); see also H. Svi Shapiro and David E. Purpel, eds., *Critical Social Issues in American Education* (New York: Longman, 1993).

Chapter Three

1. David A. Diamond, "The First Amendment and Public Schools: The Case against Judicial Intervention," *Texas Law Review* 59 (1981): p. 477.

2. Tyll van Geel, "The Search for Constitutional Limits and Governmental Authority to Inculcate Youth," *Texas Law Review* 62, no. 2 (1983): p. 197. (Van Geel argues that the Supreme Court should protect students from any effort by public schools to inculcate them with political ideas, attitudes, viewpoints, ideologies, values, or beliefs [p. 239].)

3. See, for example, William G. Buss, "School Newspapers, Public

Forum, and the First Amendment," *Iowa Law Review* 74, no. 3 (1989): pp. 505–43.

4. For wide-ranging discussions of these positions, see Thomas I. Emerson, *Toward a General Theory of the First Amendment* (New York: Random House, 1966), and Frederick Schauer, *Free Speech: A Philosophical Enquiry* (New York: Cambridge University Press, 1982).

5. Two examinations of free-speech theories have been particularly helpful to this discussion: Lee C. Bollinger, *The Tolerant Society* (New York: Oxford University Press, 1986), and Schauer, *Free Speech*.

6. John Stuart Mill, *"Utilitarianism," "On Liberty," and "Considerations on Representative Government,"* ed. H. B. Acton (New York: E. P. Dutton, 1972), pp. 111–12.

7. *Abrams v. United States,* 250 U.S. 616, 630 (Supreme Court of the United States, 1919) (Holmes, J., joined by Brandeis, J.: dissenting).

8. Mill, *"Utilitarianism," "On Liberty," and "Considerations,"* p. 79.

9. Alexander Meiklejohn, *Free Speech and Its Relation to Self-Government* (Port Washington, N.Y.: Kennikat Press, 1948).

10. Ibid., p. 88.

11. See, for example, C. Edwin Baker, "Scope of the First Amendment Freedom of Speech," *U.C.L.A. Law Review* 25 (1978): pp. 964–1040; see also: Martin H. Redish, *Freedom of Expression* (Charlottesville, Va.: Michie, 1984); and T. M. Scanlon, "Freedom of Expression and Categories of Expression," *University of Pittsburgh Law Review* 40, no. 4 (1979): pp. 517–50.

12. See, for example, Scanlon, "Freedom of Expression."

13. See, for example, Glenn Tinder, *Tolerance: Toward a New Civility* (Amherst: University of Massachusetts Press, 1975), chap. 1; see also Bollinger, *The Tolerant Society,* pp. 160–74.

14. Mark G. Yudof, *When Government Speaks* (Berkeley and Los Angeles: University of California Press, 1983), p. 105.

15. Schauer, *Free Speech,* chap. 6.

16. Mill, *"Utilitarianism," "On Liberty," and "Considerations,"* p. 102.

17. William Haley, "What Standards for Broadcasting?" *Measure* 1 (1950): pp. 211–12; cited in Schauer, *Free Speech,* pp. 75–76.

18. For an example of the "safety valve" argument, see Harold J. Laski, *A Grammar of Politics* (London: Allen and Unwin, 1938), p. 121. For relevant cases, see: *Beauharnais v. Illinois,* 343 U.S. 250 (Supreme Court of the United States, 1952); *Collin v. Smith,* 447 F.Supp. 676 (District Court of Northern Illinois, 1978), affirmed 578 F.2d 1197 (Circuit Court of Appeals, Seventh Circuit, 1978); and *Sambo's Restaurants, Inc. v. City of Ann Arbor,* 663 F.2d 686 (Circuit Court of Appeals, Sixth Circuit, 1981).

19. Schauer, *Free Speech*.

20. Ibid. ("Freedom of speech is based in large part on a distrust of the ability of government to make the necessary distinctions, a distrust of governmental determinations of truth and falsity, an appreciation of the fallibility of political leaders, and a somewhat deeper distrust of governmental power in a more general sense. It is possible to use such arguments to justify a general limitation of government, but I make no such argument here. I am arguing only that the power of government to regulate speech should, for a number of reasons, be more limited than are its powers in other areas of governance" [p. 86].) Similarly, Donald Downs cautions those who wish to replace liberal free speech with a Marcusean sort of "progressive censorship"; see Donald A. Downs, *The New Politics of Pornography* (Chicago: University of Chicago Press, 1989), pp. 148–51.

21. Tinder, *Tolerance*, p. 46.

22. Quoted in Tinder, *Tolerance*, p. 43.

23. Ibid.

24. Mill, *"Utilitarianism," "On Liberty," and "Considerations."*

25. For alternative critiques of liberal theory, see, for example, Robert Paul Wolff, Barrington Moore, Jr., and Herbert Marcuse, *A Critique of Pure Tolerance* (Boston: Beacon Press, 1965), and Michael J. Perry, *Morality, Politics, and Law* (New York: Oxford University Press, 1988).

26. Tinder, *Tolerance*, p. 16.

27. Ibid., p. 19.

28. Ibid.

29. Ibid., p. 27.

30. Ibid., p. 29.

31. Schauer, *Free Speech*, p. 26.

32. See, for example, Étienne Gilson, *The Christian Philosophy of St. Thomas Aquinas*, trans. L. K. Shook (New York: Random House, 1956); cited in Tinder, *Tolerance*.

33. Tinder, *Tolerance*, p. 31.

34. Ibid., p. 32.

35. Ibid., p. 44.

36. Ibid.

37. *Brown v. Board of Education of Topeka*, 347 U.S. 483 (Supreme Court of the United States, 1954).

38. John I. Goodlad, *A Place Called School* (New York: McGraw-Hill, 1984). The goals Goodlad speaks of are those typically embraced by educators, legislators, parents, and the general populace.

According to some critics of public education, public schools advance a "hidden curriculum" that teaches hierarchy, not democracy; it involves constant surveillance of students and egoistic competition for grades. In sum, students cannot learn democracy in the school because the school is not a democratic place. See, for example, Michael Apple and Nance R. King, "What Do Schools Teach?" in Alex Molnar and John Zahorik, eds., *Curriculum Theory* (Washington, D.C.: Association for Supervision and Curriculum Development, 1977), pp. 108–27; see also David K. Cohen and Marvin Lazerson, "Education and the Corporate Order," in Jerome Karabel and A. H. Halsey, eds., *Power and Ideology in Education* (New York: Oxford University Press, 1977), pp. 133–61. For a critique of the hidden-curriculum argument, see Richard M. Merelman, "Democratic Politics and the Culture of American Education," *American Political Science Review* 74 (1980): pp. 320–24.

39. Goodlad, *A Place Called School,* pp. 51–56.

40. See, for example, Malcom M. Stewart, "The First Amendment, the Public Schools, and the Inculcation of Community Values," *Journal of Law and Education* 18, no. 1 (1989): p. 23. ("[The] process of education must inevitably be inculcative, in the sense that it will dispose students to accept some values and opinions and reject others" [p. 25].)

41. See, for example, van Geel, "The Search for Constitutional Limits." (Van Geel considers inculcation to be synonymous with indoctrination.)

42. See, for example, Michael Apple, "Ideology Reproduction and Educational Reform," *Comparative Education Review* 22 (1978): pp. 367–88; see also Samuel Bowles and Herbert Gintis, *Schooling in Capitalist America* (New York: Basic Books, 1976).

43. See, for example, Amy Gutmann, *Democratic Education* (Princeton, N.J.: Princeton University Press, 1987), pp. 42–43. (Gutmann rejects the feasibility or desirability of a morally neutral education in democratic states.)

44. Andrew Oldenquist, "Indoctrination and Societal Suicide," *Public Interest,* no. 63 (Spring 1981): p. 86.

45. See, for example, Gutmann, *Democratic Education.*

46. See, for example, Alison G. Myhra, "The Hate Speech Conundrum and the Public Schools," *North Dakota Law Review* 68, no. 1 (1992): pp. 116–17. ("The line between permissible value inculcation and impermissible indoctrination may not be as sharp as we would prefer. Nevertheless, encouraging students to embrace certain moral norms and ideals based upon principles essential to civilized society clearly falls on the side of constitutionally permissible value inculcation. Teaching the constitutional values of equality and freedom from discrimination, along with the derivative value of mutual respect for all people, fosters pluralism and is far removed from the narrow political, religious, and moral indoctrination that the Su-

preme Court has repudiated.") See also Gerald Grant, "Children's Rights and Adult Confusions," *Public Interest,* no. 69 (Fall 1982), pp. 83–99.

47. Bruce C. Hafen, "Developing Student Expression through Institutional Authority: Public Schools as Mediating Structures," *Ohio State Law Journal* 48, no. 3 (1987): p. 668.

48. See, for example, *New York Times v. Sullivan,* 376 U.S. 254 (Supreme Court of the United States, 1964); see also *Cohen v. California,* 403 U.S. 15 (Supreme Court of the United States, 1971).

49. William K. Muir, "Teachers' Regulation of the Classroom," in David L. Kirp and Donald N. Jensen, eds., *School Days, Rule Days* (Philadelphia: Falmer Press, 1986), p. 110.

50. *Bethel School Dist. No. 403 v. Fraser,* 106 S.Ct. 3159, 3164 (Supreme Court of the United States, 1986) (Burger, C. J. concurring).

51. Myhra, "The Hate Speech Conundrum," p. 109.

52. Walter A. Kamiat, "State Indoctrination and the Protection of Non-State Voices in the Schools: Justifying a Prohibition of School Library Censorship," *Stanford Law Review* 35, no. 2 (1983): p. 517.

Chapter Four

1. Laurence H. Tribe, *American Constitutional Law,* 2d ed. (Mineola, N.Y.: Foundation Press, 1988), p. 789.

2. Daniel A. Farber and John E. Nowak, "The Misleading Nature of Public Forum Analysis: Content and Context in First Amendment Adjudication," *Virginia Law Review* 70, no. 5 (1984): p. 1235.

3. Ibid., p. 1236.

4. Tribe, *American Constitutional Law,* p. 837. ("The notion that some expression may be regulated consistent with the first amendment without meeting any separate compelling-interest test starts with the already familiar proposition that expression has special value only in the context of 'dialogue': communication in which the participants seek to persuade, or are persuaded; communication which is about changing or maintaining beliefs, or taking or refusing to take action on the basis of one's beliefs.")

5. See, for example, *Brandenburg v. Ohio,* 395 U.S. 444 (Supreme Court of the United States, 1969).

6. Tribe, *American Constitutional Law,* p. 790.

7. Farber and Nowak, "Misleading Nature of Public Forum Analysis," p. 1238.

8. Tribe, *American Constitutional Law,* p. 979.

9. Ibid.

10. According to Tribe, the seminal case was *Schneider v. State,* 308

U.S. 147 (Supreme Court of the United States, 1939) (invalidating restrictions on door-to-door distribution of circulars, and bans on their street distribution, when legitimate governmental purposes could be at least approximately achieved by less restrictive alternatives). See also *Grayned v. Rockford*, 408 U.S. 104 (Supreme Court of the United States, 1972), and *Clark v. Community*, 468 U.S. 288 (Supreme Court of the United States, 1984) (upholding facially neutral National Park Service anticamping regulations as applied to forbid protesters who wished to call attention to the plight of the homeless from sleeping in symbolic tents erected in Lafayette Park, across the street from the White House).

11. Farber and Nowak, "Misleading Nature of Public Forum Analysis," p. 1225.

12. Ibid.

13. Tribe, *American Constitutional Law*, p. 954.

14. *Perry Educ. Assn. v. Perry Local Educator's Assn.* 460 U.S. 37 (Supreme Court of the United States, 1983).

15. Ibid., p. 45.

16. Tribe, *American Constitutional Law*, p. 955.

17. Ibid.

18. See, for example, *Tinker v. Des Moines Independent Community School District*, 393 U.S. 503 (Supreme Court of the United States, 1969).

19. See, for example, *Shanley v. Northeast Ind. Sch. Dist., Bexar County, Tex.*, 462 F.2d 960 (Circuit Court of Appeals, Fifth Circuit, 1972).

20. Farber and Nowak, "Misleading Nature of Public Forum Analysis," p. 1225.

21. Ibid. (Other scholars have been critical of public forum analysis as well. See, for example, Tribe, *American Constitutional Law*, p. 993; see also Lillian R. BeVier, "Rehabilitating Public Forum Doctrine: In Defense of Categories," *Supreme Court Review, 1992* [Chicago: University of Chicago Press, 1993]), pp. 79–122.

22. See, for example, *United States v. Grace*, 461 U.S. 171 (Supreme Court of the United States, 1983); see also *Greer v. Spock*, 424 U.S. 828 (Supreme Court of the United States, 1976).

23. See, for example, *Student Coalition for Peace v. Lower Merion Sch. D.*, 596 F.Supp. 169 (District Court of Pennsylvania, 1984) (regarding such school facilities as recreational fields, stadiums, etc.); see also: *Hazelwood School Dist. v. Kuhlmeier*, 108 S.Ct. 562 (Supreme Court of the United States, 1988) (concerning censorship of a school-sponsored student newspaper); and *Perry Educ. Assn. v. Perry Local Educator's Assn.*, 460 U.S. 37 (Supreme Court of the United States, 1983) (addressed dispute over access to interschool faculty mail system).

24. See, for example, BeVier, "Rehabilitating Public Forum Doctrine," p. 122. ("If a reigning conception of the First Amendment requires judges to perform tasks that they cannot succeed in performing, First Amendment doctrine risks becoming no more than a rhetorical facade, shielding from view that its guarantee of an 'uninhibited, robust and wide-open' public debate is an empty one.")

25. Farber and Nowak, "Misleading Nature of Public Forum Analysis," p. 1240.

26. Ibid.

27. Ibid., p. 1241.

28. Ibid.

29. Ibid., p. 1243.

30. Ibid.

31. Ibid.

32. Ibid., p. 1262.

33. Ibid., p. 1266.

34. *In re Gault*, 387 U.S. 1 (Supreme Court of the United States, 1967).

35. Thomas J. Flygare, "Is *Tinker* Dead?" *Phi Delta Kappan* 68, no. 2 (1986): 165–66.

36. 258 F.Supp. 971 (District Court of Iowa, 1966).

37. 383 F.2d 988 (Circuit Court of Appeals, Eighth Circuit, 1967).

38. *Tinker v. Des Moines Independent Community School District*, 393 U.S. 503 (Supreme Court of the United States, 1969).

39. Ibid., p. 508.

40. Ibid., p. 507.

41. Ibid., p. 513.

42. Ibid., p. 507.

43. Ibid., p. 526.

44. Ibid., p. 517.

45. Ibid., p. 525.

46. Ibid., p. 520.

47. Ibid., p. 511.

48. Bruce C. Hafen, "Developing Student Expression through Institutional Authority: Public Schools as Mediating Structures," *Ohio State Law Journal* 48, no. 3 (1987): pp. 702–9.

49. Thomas I. Emerson, *Toward a General Theory of the First Amendment* (New York: Random House, 1966), p. 91.

50. *West Virginia State Board of Education v. Barnette*, 319 U.S. 624, at 637 (Supreme Court of the United States, 1943) (quoted in *Tinker v. Des Moines Independent Community School District*, 393 U.S. 503, 507 [Supreme Court of the United States, 1969]).

51. *Tinker v. Des Moines Independent Community School District,* 393 U.S. 503, 511 (Supreme Court of the United States, 1969).

52. Ibid.

53. *Keyishian v. Board of Regents of University of State of New York,* 385 U.S. 589, 603 (Supreme Court of the United States, 1967) (quoted in *Tinker v. Des Moines Independent Community School District,* 393 U.S. 503, 512 [Supreme Court of the United States, 1969]).

54. *Tinker v. Des Moines Independent Community School District,* 393 U.S. 503, 513 (Supreme Court of the United States, 1969).

55. Ibid., p. 508.

56. Ibid.

57. Ibid., p. 513.

58. Farber and Nowak, "Misleading Nature of Public Forum Analysis," p. 1246.

59. *Tinker v. Des Moines Independent Community School District,* 393 U.S. 503, 506 (Supreme Court of the United States, 1969).

60. See, for example, *Nitzberg v. Parks,* 525 F.2d 378 (Circuit Court of Appeals, Fourth Circuit, 1975); see also *Pliscou v. Holtville Unified School Dist.,* 411 F.Supp. 842 (District Court of California, 1976).

61. *Tinker v. Des Moines Independent Community School District,* 393 U.S. 503, 505 (Supreme Court of the United States, 1969).

62. Ibid., pp. 507–8.

63. The specific cases mentioned in this and subsequent chapters are drawn from a database of scores of federal court decisions handed down between 1969 and 1991. This database was derived from books, journals, legal indexes, and court decisions. I utilize particular cases for multiple purposes. They illustrate certain points relevant to my argument and analysis; they also demonstrate the feasibility of that argument, as well as its limitations and problems. It is not my intent, however, to provide an exhaustive empirical analysis of lower court decisions following *Tinker.* Given the scores of cases, invariably one can find a particular ruling that contradicts or challenges any particular point of argument. Thus, I employ them primarily for illustration, rather than as a basis for empirical conclusions regarding the development of student free speech.

64. *Tate v. Board of Ed. of Jonesboro, Ark., Spec. Sch. Dist.,* 453 F.2d 975, 978 (Circuit Court of Appeals, Eighth Circuit, 1972).

65. *Tinker v. Des Moines Independent Community School District,* 393 U.S. 503, 508 (Supreme Court of the United States, 1969).

66. *Gebert v. Hoffman,* 336 F.Supp. 694, 697 (District Court of Pennsylvania, 1972).

67. Ibid.

68. *Schwartz v. Schuker,* 298 F.Supp. 238 (District Court of New York, 1969).

69. Ibid., p. 241.

70. See, for example, *Tate v. Board of Ed. of Jonesboro, Ark., Spec. Sch. Dist.,* 453 F.2d 975 (Circuit Court of Appeals, Eighth Circuit, 1972); see also: *Gebert v. Hoffman,* 336 F.Supp. 694 (District Court of Pennsylvania, 1972); and *Schwartz v. Schuker,* 298 F.Supp. 238 (District Court of New York, 1969).

Chapter Five

1. *Sullivan v. Houston Independent School District,* 307 F.Supp. 1328 (District Court of Texas, 1969).

2. Ibid., p. 1345.

3. Ibid.

4. *Jacobs v. Board of School Commissioners,* 490 F.2d 601, 604 (Circuit Court of Appeals, Seventh Circuit, 1973).

5. Ibid., p. 605.

6. *Eisner v. Stamford Board of Education,* 440 F.2d 803 (Circuit Court of Appeals, Second Circuit, 1971).

7. Ibid., p. 805.

8. Ibid., p. 808.

9. Ibid.

10. *Bystrom v. Fridley,* 822 F.2d 747 (Circuit Court of Appeals, Eighth Circuit, 1987).

11. Ibid., p. 750.

12. *Sullivan v. Houston Independent School District,* 307 F.Supp. 1328, 1344 (District Court of Texas, 1969).

13. Compare the courts' efforts to apply the void-for-vagueness doctrine to restrictions upon adult speech. See, for example, *Cohen v. California,* 403 U.S. 15 (Supreme Court of the United States, 1971); see also: *Gooding v. Wilson,* 405 U.S. 518 (Supreme Court of the United States, 1972); and American Booksellers Ass'n, Inc., v. *Hudnut,* 771 F.2d 323 (Circuit Court of Appeals, Seventh Circuit, 1985).

14. *Sullivan v. Houston Independent School District,* 307 F.Supp. 1328, 1341 (District Court of Texas, 1969).

15. *Tinker v. Des Moines Independent Community School District,* 393 U.S. 503, 510 (Supreme Court of the United States, 1969).

16. Ibid., p. 511.

17. Ibid.

18. Lee C. Bollinger, *The Tolerant Society* (New York: Oxford University Press, 1986), p. 11.

19. This is hardly surprising, for the similarities between an economic market and an intellectual market are striking. See Bollinger, *The Tolerant Society*, p. 239.

20. Alexander Meiklejohn, *Free Speech and Its Relation to Self-Government* (Port Washington, N.Y.: Kennikat Press, 1948).

21. Victor Blasi, "The Checking Value in First Amendment Theory," *American Bar Foundation Research Journal* (1977): p. 521.

22. Frederick Schauer, *Free Speech: A Philosophical Enquiry* (New York: Cambridge University Press, 1982), pp. 80–86.

23. Ibid., p. 82.

24. Bollinger, *The Tolerant Society*, chap. 5.

25. William K. Muir, "Teachers' Regulation of the Classroom," in David L. Kirp and Donald N. Jensen, eds., *School Days, Rule Days* (Philadelphia: Falmer Press, 1986).

26. John Stuart Mill, *"Utilitarianism," "On Liberty,"* and *"Considerations on Representative Government,"* ed. H. B. Acton (New York: E. P. Dutton, 1972), p. 170.

27. David L. Kirp, "Proceduralism and Bureaucracy: Due Process in the School Setting," *Stanford Law Review* 28 (1976): p. 858.

28. John Goodlad, *A Place Called School* (New York: McGraw-Hill, 1984).

29. Alec M. Gallup, The Eighteenth Annual Gallup Poll of the Public's Attitudes toward the Public Schools (Bloomington, Ind.: Phi Delta Kappa Research Foundation, 1986). ERIC ED 283928.

30. See, for example, *Tinker v. Des Moines Independent Community School District*, 393 U.S. 503 (Supreme Court of the United States, 1969) (Black, J.: dissenting).

31. Ibid., pp. 524–25.

32. Bollinger, *The Tolerant Society*, p. 11.

33. For general discussion of this point, see Bollinger, *The Tolerant Society.*

34. Tyll van Geel, *The Courts and American Education Law* (Buffalo, N.Y.: Prometheus Books, 1987).

35. Bruce C. Hafen, "Developing Student Expression through Institutional Authority: Public Schools as Mediating Structures," *Ohio State Law Journal* 48 (1987): pp. 663–731.

36. *Thomas v. Board of Ed., Granville Cent. Sch. Dist.*, 607 F.2d 1043 (Circuit Court of Appeals, Second Circuit, 1979) (Newman, J.: concurring).

37. *Cohen v. California,* 403 U.S. 15 (Supreme Court of the United States, 1971).

38. *Scoville v. Board of Ed. of Joliet TP. H.S. Dist. 204, etc., Ill.,* 425 F.2d 10 (Circuit Court of Appeals, Seventh Circuit, 1970). ("This attempt to amuse comes as a shock to an older generation. But today's students in high school are not insulated from the shocking but legally accepted language used by demonstrators and protestors in streets and on campuses and by authors of best-selling modern literature" [p. 14]).

39. Ibid.

40. *Williams v. Spencer,* 622 F.2d 1200, 1205 (Circuit Court of Appeals, Fourth Circuit, 1980).

41. Ibid.

42. Ibid., p. 1206.

43. Ibid.

Chapter Six

1. This point is consistent with Isaiah Berlin's distinction between the "positive liberty of self-realization" and the "negative liberty of non-interference." See Isaiah Berlin, *Four Essays on Liberty* (New York: Oxford University Press, 1969), p. lvii.

2. *Hazelwood School Dist. v. Kuhlmeier,* 108 S.Ct. 562 (Supreme Court of the United States, 1988).

3. See, for example, *Garvin v. Rosenau,* 455 F.2d 233 (Circuit Court of Appeals, Sixth Circuit, 1972); see also: *Bayer v. Kinzler,* 383 F.Supp. 1164 (District Court of New York, 1974); and *Trachtman v. Anker,* 426 F.Supp. 198 (District Court of New York, 1976).

4. See, for example, *Gambino v. Fairfax Cty. Sch. Bd.,* 429 F.Supp. 731 (District Court of Virginia, 1977); see also: *Stanton by Stanton v. Brunswick School Dept.,* 577 F.Supp. 1560 (District Court of Maine, 1984); and *Student Coalition for Peace v. Lower Merion Sch. D.,* 596 F.Supp. 169 (District Court of Pennsylvania, 1984).

5. *Gambino v. Fairfax Cty. Sch. Bd.,* 429 F.Supp. 731 (District Court of Virginia, 1977).

6. Ibid., p. 734.

7. Ibid., p. 735.

8. *Student Coalition for Peace v. Lower Merion Sch. D.,* 596 F.Supp. 169, 173 (District Court of Pennsylvania, 1984).

9. Ibid.

10. Ibid., p. 173.

11. *Gambino v. Fairfax Cty. Sch. Bd.,* 429 F.Supp. 731, 735 (District Court of Virginia, 1977).

12. *Hazelwood School Dist. v. Kuhlmeier,* 108 S.Ct. 562 (Supreme Court of the United States, 1988).

13. Ibid., p. 568.

14. See, for example, *Quarterman v. Byrd,* 453 F.2d 54, 59 (Circuit Court of Appeals, Fourth Circuit, 1971); see also *Baughman v. Freienmuth,* 478 F.2d 1345, 1348, 1351 (Circuit Court of Appeals, Fourth Circuit, 1973).

15. *Stanton by Stanton v. Brunswick School Dept.,* 577 F.Supp. 1560, 1573 (District Court of Maine, 1984).

16. *Baughman v. Freienmuth,* 478 F.2d 1345, 1350 (Circuit Court of Appeals, Fourth Circuit, 1973).

17. *Quarterman v. Byrd,* 453 F.2d 54 (Circuit Court of Appeals, Fourth Circuit, 1971).

18. *Baughman v. Freienmuth,* 478 F.2d 1345, 1351 (Circuit Court of Appeals, Fourth Circuit, 1973).

19. *Stanton by Stanton v. Brunswick School Dept.,* 577 F.Supp. 1560, 1574 (District Court of Maine, 1984).

20. Ibid., p. 1575 ("If the intellectual and ideological ferment of the last four decades of the American social experience teaches anything, it teaches us that whatever may be the accepted meaning of 'good taste' on any given day, the content of that meaning does not rigidly abide through time").

21. *Hazelwood School Dist. v. Kuhlmeier,* 108 S.Ct. 562, 574 (Supreme Court of the United States, 1988) (Brennan, J.: dissenting).

22. *Nitzberg v. Parks,* 525 F.2d 378, 383 (Circuit Court of Appeals, Fourth Circuit, 1975).

23. *Baughman v. Freienmuth,* 478 F.2d 1345, 1349 (Circuit Court of Appeals, Fourth Circuit, 1973) (original quote: *Interstate Circuit, Inc. v. Dallas,* 390 U.S. 676, 689 [Supreme Court of the United States, 1968]).

24. *Bethel School Dist. No. 403 v. Fraser,* 106 S.Ct. 3159, 3169 (Supreme Court of the United States, 1986) (Stevens, J.: dissenting). ("If a student is to be punished for using offensive speech, he is entitled to fair notice of the scope of the prohibition and the consequences of its violation. The interest in free speech protected by the First Amendment and the interest in fair procedure protected by the Due Process Clause of the Fourteenth Amendment combine to require this conclusion.")

25. For a constitutional parallel, we may look to *Goss v. Lopez,* 419 U.S. 565 (Supreme Court of the United States, 1975) (imposing a modicum of due process regarding school suspensions).

26. *Hazelwood School Dist. v. Kuhlmeier,* 108 S.Ct. 562 (Supreme Court of the United States, 1988).

27. Ibid., p. 570.

28. Ibid.

29. Ibid., p. 566.

30. *Bethel School Dist. No. 403 v. Fraser,* 106 S.Ct. 3159, 3164 (Supreme Court of the United States, 1986).

31. David A. Diamond, "The First Amendment and Public Schools: The Case against Judicial Intervention," *Texas Law Review* 59 (1981): p. 485.

32. *Bethel School Dist. No. 403 v. Fraser,* 106 S.Ct. 3159, 3167 (Supreme Court of the United States, 1986).

33. *Bethel School Dist. No. 403 v. Fraser,* 755 F.2d 1356 (Circuit Court of Appeals, Ninth Circuit, 1985).

34. *Bethel School Dist. No. 403 v. Fraser,* 106 S.Ct. 3159 (Supreme Court of the United States, 1986).

35. Ibid., p. 3163.

36. Ibid., p. 3166.

37. Ibid., p. 3166–72.

38. *Hazelwood School Dist. v. Kuhlmeier,* 607 F.Supp. 1450 (District Court of Missouri, 1985).

39. *Hazelwood School Dist. v. Kuhlmeier,* 795 F.2d 1368 (Circuit Court of Appeals, Eighth Circuit, 1986).

40. *Hazelwood School Dist. v. Kuhlmeier,* 108 S.Ct. 562, 568 (Supreme Court of the United States, 1988).

41. Ibid., p. 571.

42. Ibid., p. 570.

43. Ibid.

44. Ibid.

45. Ibid.

46. Ibid., pp. 573–80 (Brennan, J.: dissenting).

47. Ibid., p. 577 (Brennan, J.: dissenting).

48. Ibid., p. 580.

49. Ibid., p. 576.

50. Ibid., p. 580.

51. These two decisions have received considerable scholarly criticism. See, for example, Larry Bartlett and Linda Frost, "The Closing of the School House Gates: Increasing Restrictions on the Public School Student's Exercise of Speech and Expression," *Thurgood Marshall Law Review* 16 (1991): 311–32, and Dinita L. James, "The School as Publisher: *Hazelwood School District v. Kuhlmeier,*" *North Carolina Law Review* 67, no. 2 (1989): pp. 503–16.

52. *Augustus v. School Board of Escambia County,* 361 F.Supp. 383 (District Court of Florida, 1973).

53. Ibid., p. 385.

54. Ibid., p. 386.

55. Ibid., p. 388.

56. Ibid.

57. *Bethel School Dist. No. 403 v. Fraser,* 106 S.Ct. 3159, 3165 (Supreme Court of the United States, 1986).

58. *Frasca v. Andrews,* 463 F.Supp. 1043, 1046 (District Court of New York, 1979).

59. Ibid.

60. *Gambino v. Fairfax Cty. Sch. Bd.,* 429 F.Supp. 731, 736 (District Court of Virginia, 1977).

61. *Hazelwood School Dist. v. Kuhlmeier,* 108 S.Ct. 562, 576 (Supreme Court of the United States, 1988) (Brennan, J.: dissenting).

62. Ibid., p. 570.

63. *Stanton by Stanton v. Brunswick School Dept.,* 577 F.Supp. 1560 (District Court of Maine, 1984).

64. Ibid., p. 1561.

65. Ibid., p. 1566.

66. Ibid., p. 1562.

67. Ibid.

68. Ibid., pp. 1574–75.

69. Ibid., p. 1574. ("Rejection of Plaintiff's designated quotation on the basis of a standard of 'poor taste' or 'appropriateness' either to the yearbook or to some narrow segment of public opinion, such as Brunswick High School seniors, or to a wider segment, such as the populace of Brunswick, fixes no discrete, objective limits to the determination of what may or may not be published therein. That test must always be, by such standards, completely subjective in at least two respects; what the official making the decision as to publishability thinks to be 'tasteful' or 'appropriate' and what that official believes others may think to be so.")

70. Ibid., p. 1571.

71. *Hazelwood School Dist. v. Kuhlmeier,* 108 S.Ct. 562, 579 (Supreme Court of the United States, 1988) (Brennan, J.: dissenting).

72. See, for example, *Rust v. Sullivan,* 111 S.Ct. 1759 (Supreme Court of the United States, 1991). (The Court upheld Department of Health and Human Services regulations prohibiting Title X projects from engaging in abortion counseling, referral, and activities advocating abortion as a method of family planning.)

73. *Hazelwood School Dist. v. Kuhlmeier,* 108 S.Ct. 562, 570 (Supreme Court of the United States, 1988) (Brennan, J.: dissenting).

Chapter Seven

1. See, for example: *Minarcini v. Strongsville City School Dist.*, 541 F.2d 577 (Circuit Court of Appeals, Sixth Circuit, 1976); *Right to Read Defense Com. v. School Com., etc.*, 454 F.Supp. 703 (District Court of Massachusetts, 1978); *Salvail v. Nashua Bd. of Ed.*, 469 F.Supp. 1269 (District Court of New Hampshire, 1979); *Zykan v. Warsaw Community School Corp.*, 631 F.2d 1300 (Circuit Court of Appeals, Seventh Circuit, 1980); *Bicknell v. Vergennes Union High School Bd., etc.*, 638 F.2d 438 (Circuit Court of Appeals, Second Circuit, 1980); *Sheck v. Baileyville School Committee*, 530 F.Supp. 679 (District Court of Maine, 1982); *Board of Educ., Island Trees Union Free School Dist. No. 26 v. Pico*, 457 U.S. 853 (Supreme Court of the United States, 1982).

2. *Board of Educ., Island Trees Union Free School Dist. No. 26 v. Pico*, 457 U.S. 853, 857 (Supreme Court of the United States, 1982).

3. Ibid., p. 858.

4. *Board of Educ., Island Trees Union Free School Dist. No. 26 v. Pico*, 474 F.Supp. 387 (District Court of New York, 1979).

5. Ibid., p. 397.

6. *Board of Educ., Island Trees Union Free School Dist. No. 26 v. Pico*, 638 F.2d 404 (Circuit Court of Appeals, Second Circuit, 1980).

7. Ibid., pp. 414–15.

8. Ibid., pp. 432–38.

9. Ibid., pp. 419–32.

10. *Board of Educ., Island Trees Union Free School Dist. No. 26 v. Pico*, 457 U.S. 853 (Supreme Court of the United States, 1982). (Justice Brennan was joined in all by Justice Marshall and Justice Stevens. Justice Blackmun joined in judgment and in part, while Justice White joined in judgment.)

11. Ibid., p. 862.

12. Ibid., p. 869.

13. Ibid., p. 866.

14. Ibid., pp. 867–68.

15. Ibid., p. 870.

16. Ibid., p. 871.

17. Ibid.

18. Ibid., p. 874.

19. Ibid., pp. 867, 871.

20. Ibid., p. 879.

21. Ibid.

22. Ibid.
23. Ibid.
24. Ibid., p. 881.
25. Ibid.
26. Ibid., p. 889.
27. Ibid., p. 891.
28. Ibid., p. 889.
29. Ibid.
30. Ibid., p. 909.
31. Ibid., p. 910.
32. Ibid., p. 911.
33. Ibid., p. 914.
34. Ibid., p. 917.
35. Ibid., p. 910.
36. Ibid., p. 915.
37. Ibid., p. 919.
38. Ibid., p. 894.
39. Ibid., p. 895.
40. *Martin v. City of Struthers*, 319 U.S. 141 (Supreme Court of the United States, 1943).
41. *Stanley v. Georgia*, 393 U.S. 557 (Supreme Court of the United States, 1969).
42. *Red Lion Broadcasting Co. v. FCC*, 395 U.S. 367 (Supreme Court of the United States, 1969).
43. *Procunier v. Martinez*, 416 U.S. 396 (Supreme Court of the United States, 1974).
44. *Virginia State Bd. of Pharmacy v. Virginia Citizens Council*, 425 U.S. 748 (Supreme Court of the United States, 1976).
45. Ibid., p. 867.
46. Ibid. ("The dissemination of ideas can accomplish nothing if otherwise willing addressees are not free to receive and consider them. It would be a barren marketplace of ideas that had only sellers and no buyers.") (Original quote in *Lamont v. Postmaster General*, 381 U.S. 301, 308 [Supreme Court of the United States, 1965] [Brennan, J.: concurring].)
47. Ibid.
48. Ibid.
49. *Right to Read Defense Com. v. School Com., etc.*, 454 F.Supp. 703, 715 (District Court of Massachusetts, 1978).
50. Martin D. Munic, "Education or Indoctrination—Removal of Books from Public School Libraries: *Board of Education, Island Trees*

Union Free School District No. 26 v. Pico," *Minnesota Law Review* 68, no. 1 (1983): 213–53 (p. 239, n. 153).

51. *Board of Educ., Island Trees Union Free School Dist. No. 26 v. Pico,* 457 U.S. 853, 862 (Supreme Court of the United States, 1982).

52. Ibid., p. 869.

53. Ibid.

54. Ibid.

55. Ibid.

56. Ibid., p. 878.

57. Ibid., p. 892. ("It is not clear, however, why this distinction requires greater scrutiny. . . . It would appear that required reading and textbooks have a greater likelihood of imposing a 'pall of orthodoxy' over the educational process than do optional reading" [Burger, C. J.: dissenting].)

58. Ibid., p. 893.

59. Ibid., p. 916.

60. *Presidents Council Dist. No. 25 v. Community Sch. Bd. No. 25,* 457 F.2d 289, 293 (Circuit Court of Appeals, Second Circuit, 1972).

61. Ibid., pp. 878–79.

62. Ibid., p. 871.

63. Ibid.

64. Ibid., p. 872.

65. Ibid., p. 917.

66. Ibid.

67. Ibid., pp. 870–71.

68. See, for example, *Presidents Council Dist. 25 v. Community Sch. Bd. No. 25,* 457 F.2d 289 (Circuit Court of Appeals, Second Circuit, 1972); see also: *Right to Read Defense Com. v. School Com., etc.,* 454 F.Supp. 703 (District Court of Massachusetts, 1978); *Bicknell v. Vergennes Union High School Bd., etc.,* 638 F.2d 438 (Circuit Court of Appeals, Second Circuit, 1980); and *Sheck v. Baileyville School Committee,* 530 F.Supp. 679 (District Court of Maine, 1982).

69. *Board of Educ., Island Trees Union Free School Dist. No. 26 v. Pico,* 457 U.S. 853, 907 (Supreme Court of the United States, 1982) (Rehnquist, J.: dissenting).

70. Ibid., p. 913.

71. Ibid., p. 915.

72. Ibid., p. 871.

73. See, in general, *Cohen v. California,* 403 U.S. 15 (Supreme Court of the United States, 1971).

74. *Board of Educ., Island Trees Union Free School Dist. No. 26 v.*

Pico, 457 U.S. 853, 890 (Supreme Court of the United States, 1982) (Burger, C. J.: dissenting).

75. Ibid., p. 897.

76. Ibid., p. 871.

77. Ibid., p. 890.

78. Ibid., p. 880.

79. Ibid., p. 866.

80. Ibid., p. 909.

81. Ibid., p. 911.

82. George F. Will, "How to Judge a Judge," *Newsweek* July 15, 1991 ("Courts do not exist to right all the wrongs that other government agencies have, for whatever reasons, refused to right. Neither the adjective 'unwise' nor even 'unjust' is a synonym for 'unconstitutional' when modifying the noun 'law'" [p. 64]).

83. *Right to Read Defense Com. v. School Com., etc.,* 454 F.Supp. 703, 705 (District Court of Massachusetts, 1978).

84. *Male and Female Under Eighteen,* compiled by Nancy Larrick and Eve Merriam (New York: Avon, 1973).

85. Ibid., p. 703.

86. Ibid., p. 707.

87. Ibid., p. 708.

88. Ibid., p. 710.

89. Ibid., p. 712.

90. Ibid., p. 713.

91. Ibid.

92. Ibid., p. 714.

93. *Board of Educ., Island Trees Union Free School Dist. No. 26 v. Pico,* 457 U.S. 853, 885 (Supreme Court of the United States, 1982) (Burger, C. J.: dissenting).

94. *Right to Read Defense Com. v. School Com., etc.,* 454 F.Supp. 703, 714 (District Court of Massachusetts, 1978).

95. *Pratt v. Ind. Sch. Dist. No. 831, Forest Lake,* 670 F.2d 771, 775 (Circuit Court of Appeals, Eighth Circuit, 1982).

96. Ibid., p. 775.

97. Ibid., p. 776.

98. Ibid.

99. Ibid., pp. 776–77.

100. Ibid., p. 717.

101. Ibid., p. 779.

102. *Board of Educ., Island Trees Union Free School Dist. No. 26 v.*

Pico, 457 U.S. 853, 914 (Supreme Court of the United States, 1982) (Rehnquist, J.: dissenting).
   103. Ibid., p. 921.

Chapter Eight

   1. William Lasser, *The Limits of Judicial Power* (Chapel Hill: University of North Carolina Press, 1988), p. 270.
   2. For effective discussions of judicial review, see, for example: John Ely, *Democracy and Distrust* (Cambridge, Mass.: Harvard University Press, 1980); and Michael Perry, *The Constitution, the Courts, and Human Rights* (New Haven, Conn.: Yale University Press, 1982). For severe criticisms of judicial review, see, for example, Raoul Berger, *Government by Judiciary* (Cambridge, Mass.: Harvard University Press, 1977). For a provocative discussion regarding capacity, see, for example, Donald L. Horowitz, *The Courts and Social Policy* (Washington, D.C.: Brookings Institution, 1977). For other criticisms see, for example, "Symposium: Judicial Review and the Constitution — The Text and Beyond," *University of Dayton Law Review* 8 (1983): p. 443; Laurence Tribe, "The Puzzling Persistence of Process-Based Constitutional Theories," *Yale Law Journal* 89 (1980): p. 1063; Mark Tushnet, "Darkness on the Edge of Town: The Contributions of John Hart Ely to Constitutional Theory," *Yale Law Journal* 89 (1980): p. 1037; and Ralph Cavanagh and Austin Sarat, "Thinking about Courts: Toward and Beyond a Jurisprudence of Judicial Competence," *Law and Society Review,* 14 (1980): p. 371.
   3. Horowitz, *The Courts and Social Policy,* p. 18.
   4. Joel B. Grossman, "Judicial Legitimacy and the Role of Courts: Shapiro's *Courts,*" *American Bar Foundation,* no. 1 (1984): pp. 214–15.
   5. Ibid.
   6. Ibid.
   7. Michael A. Rebell and Arthur R. Block, *Educational Policymaking and the Courts* (Chicago: University of Chicago Press, 1982), p. 201.
   8. Tyll van Geel, "The Search for Constitutional Limits on Governmental Authority to Inculcate Youth," *Texas Law Review* 62, no. 1 (1983): p. 291.
   9. *Hazelwood School Dist. v. Kuhlmeier,* 108 S.Ct. 562, 574 (Supreme Court of the United States, 1988) (Brennan, J.: dissenting).
   10. *Tinker v. Des Moines Independent Community School District,* 393 U.S. 503, 525 (Supreme Court of the United States, 1969) (Black, J.: dissenting).

11. Ibid., p. 517.

12. Ibid., p. 525.

13. David A. Diamond, "The First Amendment and Public Schools: The Case against Judicial Intervention," *Texas Law Review* 59 (1981): p. 528.

14. *Tinker v. Des Moines Independent Community School District,* 393 U.S. 503, 513 (Supreme Court of the United States, 1969) (original quotation in *Keyishian v. Board of Regents,* 385 U.S. 589, 603 [Supreme Court of the United States, 1967]).

15. Van Geel, "The Search for Constitutional Limits," p. 290.

16. Ibid.

17. Bruce C. Hafen, "Developing Student Expression through Institutional Authority: Public Schools as Mediating Structures," *Ohio State Law Journal* 48 (1987): p. 669.

18. Malcolm M. Stewart, "The First Amendment, the Public Schools, and the Inculcation of Community Values," *Journal of Law and Education* 18, no. 1 (1989): p. 25.

19. Ibid., pp. 26–27.

20. Robert M. Gordon, "Freedom of Expression and Values Inculcation in the Public School Curriculum," *Journal of Law and Education* 13, no. 4 (1984): p. 535.

21. Ibid., p. 536.

22. Ibid., p. 531.

23. Ibid.

24. Ibid., p. 535.

25. Ibid.

26. Stewart, "The First Amendment," p. 91.

27. William G. Buss, "School Newspapers, Public Forum, and the First Amendment," *Iowa Law Review* 74, no. 3 (1989): p. 514.

28. Mark G. Yudof, *When Government Speaks* (Berkeley and Los Angeles: University of California Press, 1983), p. 42.

29. Hillary Rodham underscores this point in her advice to child advocates. See Hillary Rodham, "Children's Rights: A Legal Perspective," in Patricia A. Vardin and Ilene N. Brady, eds., *Children's Rights: Contemporary Perspectives* (New York: Teachers College Press, 1979), p. 34. "Lawsuits are only one approach to problem solving in the law; a lawyer might instead decide to pursue administrative, legislative, or political action to achieve the objective. The children's rights movement must be as flexible and as realistic.")

30. Robert B. Keiter, "Judicial Review of Student First Amendment Claims: Assessing the Legitimacy-Capacity Debate," *Missouri Law Review* 50, no. 1 (1985): p. 56.

31. Ibid.

32. Ibid.

33. Stewart, "The First Amendment," p. 27.

34. Ibid.

35. Ibid., p. 56. ("Our nation's educational system presumes the desirability of community control over public education. While the result in particular instances may be unfortunate, the remedy lies in more broad-based participation in the political process, not in judicial circumvention of it.")

36. Ibid., p. 91.

37. *Board of Educ., Island Trees Union Free School Dist. No. 26 v. Pico,* 457 U.S. 853, 908 (Supreme Court of the United States, 1982) (Rehnquist, J.: dissenting).

38. Ibid., p. 920.

39. Joseph Tussman, *Government and the Mind* (New York: Oxford University Press, 1977), p. 8.

40. Van Geel, "The Search for Constitutional Limits," p. 262.

41. Ibid.

42. Ibid.

43. Ibid., p. 254.

44. Ibid.

45. Ibid.

46. Ibid., p. 253.

47. Van Geel is not alone in advocating a stringent level of judicial review. See, for example, Betsy Levin, "Educating Youth for Citizenship: The Conflict between Authority and Individual Rights in the Public School," *Yale Law Journal* 95, no. 8 (1986): pp. 1653–54. (Levin argues that denying substantial First Amendment rights to students undermines government authority in general, for it teaches students undesirable lessons regarding the relationship between the individual citizen and government.)

48. Hafen, "Developing Student Expression," p. 705.

49. Stewart, "The First Amendment," pp. 25–26.

50. Ibid.

51. Liam K. Grimley, "Spiritual and Moral Development," *Viewpoints in Teaching and Learning* 58, no. 2 (1982): p. 79.

52. Ibid., p. 84.

53. Andrew Oldenquist, "Indoctrination and Societal Suicide," *Public Interest* 63 (1981): pp. 84–86.

54. Tussman, *Government and the Mind,* p. 145.

55. Ibid., p. 54.

56. Ibid., pp. 10–14.

57. Amy Gutmann, *Democratic Education* (Princeton, N.J.: Princeton University Press, 1987), p. 51.

58. Yudof, *When Government Speaks,* p. 52.

59. Ibid., p. 53.

60. Ibid.

Index